CONTEMPLATION

CONTEMPLATION

An Islamic Psychospiritual Study

MALIK BADRI

With an Introduction by
SHAYKH YUSUF AL-QARADAWI

Translated from the Arabic by
ABDUL-WAHID LU'LU'A

THE INTERNATIONAL INSTITUTE OF ISLAMIC THOUGHT

THE INTERNATIONAL INSTITUTE OF ISLAMIC THOUGHT
P.O. BOX 669, HERNDON, VA 22070, USA

LONDON OFFICE
P.O. BOX 126, RICHMOND, SURREY TW9 2UD, UK

ISBN 1–56564–267–8 paperback
ISBN 1–56564–273–2 hardback

Printed in the United Kingdom
by Cambridge University Press

CONTENTS

		page
Foreword		vii
Introduction by Shaykh Yusuf al-Qaradawi		ix
Author's Introduction		xiii
1	Contemplation: A Modern Psychological Perspective	1
2	Contemplation: The Works of Early Muslim Scholars	21
3	Islamic Contemplation and Modern Meditation Procedures	36
4	The Qur'an and the Contemplation of God's Creation	53
5	Contemplation as an Unrestricted Form of Worship	64
6	Contemplation of the Invisible and its Limits	67
7	Individual Levels of Contemplation	78
8	Experimental Science and Religion: The Cosmic Laws	92
9	Conclusion	113
Notes		119
Bibliography		125
Index of Qur'anic Citations		129
General Index		130

FOREWORD

بسم الله الرحمن الرحيم

Of knowledge, we have none, save what
You have taught us. (The Qur'an 2:32)

The International Institute of Islamic Thought (IIIT) has great pleasure in presenting this treatise on Islamic psychology, which, though small in size, is rich in meaning. The author, Professor Malik Badri, is a well-known scholar who was a pioneer of the school that is striving to present psychology from an Islamic perspective, and has encouraged and inspired a number of researchers and scholars to participate in this ongoing research.

The first Arabic edition, *Al-Tafakkur min al-Mushāhadah ila al-Shuhūd*, which was published in Cairo in 1991, generated a very positive response and at times spirited remarks from scholars. Some admitted that the book had greatly improved their practice of worship and believed that it would have the same effect on others. Since then, the book has been reprinted and has been reviewed favorably in various professional journals that have considered it a best seller. It has also been used as a postgraduate reference for Islamic psychology and education in various Arab universities.

We hope that this English edition, with its ground-breaking paradigm and ideas, will not only make an important contribution to the field of the Islamization of the behavioral sciences, but also attract wider attention and generate greater interest among specialists to analyze and further develop the ideas and theories presented and discussed. Having said that, it needs to be emphasized that this is not a book for specialists, scholars and intellectuals alone, and that it provides interesting and useful reading for the general reader. Indeed it is a book for anyone who is interested in the Islamic approach towards the urgency felt by modern societies for the rediscovery of the long-forgotten and neglected spiritual aspect of their lives.

Rather than writing a new introduction for the English translation, we found that an abridged edition of the original introduction by Dr. Yusuf al-Qaradawi could serve as an excellent introduction for the English edition.

The IIIT, established in 1981, has served as a major center to facilitate sincere and serious scholarly efforts based on Islamic vision, values and principles. Its programs of research, seminars and conferences during the last nineteen years have resulted in the publication of more than two hundred and fifty titles in English and Arabic, many of which have been translated into several other languages.

We would like to express our thanks and gratitude to Professor Malik Badri, who, throughout the various stages of the book's production, co-operated closely with the editorial group at the London Office. He was very helpful in responding to our various queries, suggestions and slight amendments.

We would also like to thank the editorial and production team at the London Office and those who were directly or indirectly involved in the completion of this book: Alexandra Grayson, Sylvia Hunt, Shiraz Khan, Sohail and Sarah Nakhooda. May God reward them, the author, and the translator for all their efforts.

Shawwal 1420
January 2000

ANAS AL-SHAIKH-ALI
IIIT Translation Department
London, UK

INTRODUCTION

Praise be to God, and Prayers and Peace be upon His Messenger, and all his Companions and Followers

One of the problems of the Muslim world today is that it has become dependent on the West in all branches of modern knowledge. Those who judge religion by the behavior of the so-called religious people of today falsely attribute this to our religion or our values. However, in the past the Islamic civilization was one of the richest in the world: the universities of the Muslim world were centers of knowledge that attracted students from East and West; the books of their renowned scholars became international sources of reference; and Arabic played a fundamental role in the transmission of knowledge. This position is acknowledged by historians such as Robert Briffault, George Sarton, Gustave le Bon and Will Durant.

The pure sciences are essentially neutral because they are not affected by race, nationality, religion or culture, except maybe in their philosophy and the way in which they are taught. Human and social sciences, however, are closely connected with people, and are greatly affected by their behavior and relations, and their values and beliefs. Although some intellectuals claim that these disciplines are cross-cultural, they have nevertheless become fundamentally Western in thought and outlook, even in application, since they were initiated in the West and cater for the Western vision of life. This state of affairs represents a danger to the Islamic culture and its spiritual, moral and human values which are left largely unobserved.

Muslim specialists should therefore take an independent line in the study of these disciplines and adopt an attitude of inquiry and criticism instead of passive acceptance. They should also explore the rich cultural heritage of Islam and draw from the extensive resources available in the Qur'an, the Sunnah and the works of the outstanding people of this Ummah. Not only will this provide new useful data which can help them solve many problems faced in these disciplines but, more importantly, it will reduce the materialism, fanaticism and narrow-mindedness that some of these disciplines have acquired.

I am not suggesting that all the achievements of the West in these disciplines should be discarded and replaced by a totally new and independent field, for knowledge is like a chain where each new link comes to reinforce, correct or at least improve the other. However, no knowledge is infallible, and Muslims should be allowed to select from Western thought that which suits their norms and beliefs.

Having undergone a great change in the hands of the behaviorist school – with its developed programs, workshops, experimentations and statistics – psychology has become one of the human sciences that could benefit from the input of an Islamic perspective. Such an approach would include the study of the human soul, in its inherent potential and its observable behavior, in the light of the Qur'an and the Sunnah. It would also incorporate the ideas of some outstanding Muslim scholars who combined 'worldly' and spiritual knowledge.

In recent years, an increasing number of scholars have been contributing to what is now referred to as the 'Islamization of knowledge'. In the field of psychology, these pioneers include the Egyptian scholar Muhammad Othman Najati who published *Al-Qur'ān wa ʿIlm al-Nafs* (The Qur'an and Psychology) and *Al-Ḥadīth wa 'Ilm al-Nafs* (The Hadith and Psychology) and, in the Sudan, the author of this book, Malik Badri, who is an outstanding research psychologist, scholar and therapist. Amongst other things, he initiated a school that approaches the human psyche and its behavior from an open-minded Islamic perspective, combining traditional and contemporary knowledge. Indeed, he has treated several psychological conditions with prescribed potent cures which he deduced from Islamic practices, beliefs, morals and legal judgments. The Prophet said: "God has not created an illness without its cure; some may know it and some may not"[1] – a saying that can be applied to psychological as well as physical illnesses.

In this work, *Contemplation: An Islamic Psychospiritual Study* (*Al-Tafakkur min al-Mushāhadah ilā al-Shuhūd*), Badri approaches a highly important subject from both an Islamic and a modern psychological perspective. The Arabic title, which can be translated as 'Contemplation from perception to spiritual cognition', reveals the author's intention to progress from the stage of sensory perception, which is the basis of experimental science, to the stage of cognition and insight which is implied by the Prophet in his explanation of *iḥsān*: "It is when you worship God knowing that, even if you cannot see Him, He sees you."[2]

The author examines the Islamic injunction to contemplate and judge according to the guidance of honest and calm thought. Indeed, the Qur'an says: "I admonish you on one point: that you stand before God, in pairs or alone, and reflect..." (34:46).[3]

Badri also examines the meaning and importance of contemplation as a form of worship. It is reported that Ibn ʿAbbās said, "One hour of contemplation is better than a whole night of vigil in worship," while other authorities also said that, "One hour of contemplation is better than a whole year of worship." Furthermore, contemplation is a free form of worship which, short of contemplation of the Divine Being Himself, is not hindered by any limitation of space or time, or any obstacles, seen or unseen. In his endeavor to distinguish Islamic contemplation from other forms of meditation, Badri compares it to thinking and especially transcendental meditation which has achieved much following in the West in recent years. However, he suggests that when Muslims contemplate the creation, the self and the laws of the Almighty therein, they excel over other contemplators because they have higher incentives and expectations from God.

In this work, the author has chosen to liberate himself from the pressures of the behaviorist school of psychology which was established by J. B. Watson and is endorsed by many universities and research centers. The behaviorist school reduces all human intellectual and complex activities to a series of stimuli and responses, in order to turn psychology into a strictly experimental science. They have even gone so far as to consider human beings as mere instruments that simply need to be exposed to certain environmental stimuli in order to obtain the responses expected by the researcher. Badri criticizes this approach, confirming what the famous British scholar Cyril Burt said, namely, that modern psychology had lost its mind after having lost both its soul and its consciousness. Indeed, for psychology to be an experimental science, the behaviorists present humans as being totally devoid of conscious feelings as well as any intricate mental, intellectual or spiritual essence.

The author also denounces the attempt of the materialists to turn psychology into a material science, like physics or chemistry, because he believes strongly that, unlike matter, human beings cannot be controlled. He refutes their claim that the thinking mind is nothing but reflections of the inherent changes in the chemistry of the brain and its electrochemical reactions. In doing so, Badri has made use of the achievements of cognitive psychology which override all the schools that tried to imprison human behavior in a narrow theoretical impasse, and proves what was already established by Islam: namely, that contemplation of the signs of God, of the self, and of creation, is central to an individual's faith and is the source of every good deed.

This book is an example of how the human sciences can support faith and spiritual values, and how, when a mind is guided by the Qur'an and the Sunnah, it will be graced by the light of faith and the light of revelation, as well as the guiding light of reason. May God reward the author for his efforts.

YUSUF AL-QARADAWI
Doha, Qatar

AUTHOR'S INTRODUCTION

This book is in many ways very different from the original written in Arabic, as I have updated and rectified some of its content, including the title, and have added new material amounting to more than fifty-two pages – almost half its original size.

Writing for English readers requires a slight change in content and style because of having to produce a faithful translation of the verses of the Qur'an and the sayings of the Prophet Muhammad (ṢAAS);[1] this also applies to quotations of beautiful Arabic prose and poetry. Indeed, Arabic is a very articulate language with words and expressions that are not found in English. For example, I could not find an exact English equivalent for a number of religiously-oriented Arabic terms that describe subtle inner emotions such as *khushūᶜ*. This term, which originates from the verb *khashaᶜa,* refers to a state of total humility to the extent of becoming motionless, silent, fearful and subservient. For the Muslim, it carries the sentiments of emotional appreciation of the greatness of God mixed with love, submission and fear. In Arabic–English dictionaries it is often translated simply as 'submission', although 'submission' in Arabic is *istislām* and not *khushūᶜ*, since a person may fully submit to a forceful power without loving it or appreciating its magnificence; he may even hate it! Thus *khushūᶜ* will, by necessity, include submission, but the opposite is not true. Another example of a possible confusion due to translation is the verb *yaghbiṭ*. In Arabic it means that one admits to oneself that somebody else is better in a certain way, that one envies them and strongly wishes to be like them, but without wanting to deprive them of what they have. This is considered a good emotion. However, if one's feelings are destructive and include a desire for the other person to lose what they have, then the Arabic term used is *ḥasad*, and is considered to be a sinful emotion. The fine differentiation between these good and evil emotions is not found in English where no word exists to express a kind of jealousy that is positive, or at least not sinful. Therefore I had to rewrite many passages in order to make sure that my thoughts were portrayed correctly.

Tafakkur, which is the central theme of this book, also does not have a precise English translation. The two words that are closest to it in meaning, namely 'meditation' and 'contemplation', do not give the term *tafakkur* its true Islamic religious dimension. As the reader will see throughout this study, *tafakkur*, like contemplation and meditation, involves deep thinking and reflection, but the aim of this meditative contemplation is necessarily spiritual in nature. It is a refined form of worshipping God by appreciating His creation in His vast universe. The words 'contemplation' and 'meditation' are frequently used as synonyms in English dictionaries, although meditation is usually reserved for contemplation in spiritual matters. However, the term 'meditation' has been so often used in relation to the spirituality of Eastern religions that its use to explain *tafakkur* can be misleading. This is particularly the case when we know that the meditative procedures of Eastern religions tend to sacrifice conscious sober thinking in order to obtain altered states of consciousness, whereas *tafakkur* as an Islamic form of worship is a cognitive spiritual activity in which the rational mind, emotion and spirit must be combined. It is for this reason that I have preferred to use 'contemplation' rather than 'meditation' in the title of the book. It should also be stated that whenever words such as contemplation, meditation, reflection, deep thinking, cogitation or similar terms are used, they are simply the nearest terms available to express *tafakkur*.

I have intentionally avoided detailing definitions and intricate semantic differences of a few other Arabic terms, like spirit (*rūḥ*), soul (*nafs*) and heart (*qalb*), because this would require a whole volume in itself and would detract the reader from the simple message that I wish to convey. Although I do not subscribe to al-Ghazālī's conception that all these terms refer to only one spiritual entity and that the different names stand for the different functions that it performs, I have nevertheless adopted it in this book.

I wish to conclude by expressing my indebtedness to the IIIT office in Khartoum, Sudan, who allowed me to use the library resources for writing the original Arabic edition. In particular, I would like to mention the director, Abdallah Makki, and Mrs. Sittana Hamad, who wrote the whole book by hand from my dictation, as in the 1980s neither of us was computer literate!

I would also like to express my gratitude towards Shaykh Yusuf al-Qaradawi, the scholar and internationally known author, who honored me by accepting my request to write an introduction to this book.

I am grateful to IIIT for deciding that my work should be translated into English, and the London Office for their hard work in copy-editing and bringing my attention to missing references and points needing to be clarified. I am also very grateful to Professor Abdul-Wahid Lu'lu'a for taking on the difficult task of translating my work.

Finally, I wish to dedicate this book to the blessed souls of three women who shaped my life: my mother Nafisa and my two aunts Maymoona and Sakina.

Dhu al-Qaᶜdah 1419
March 1999

MALIK BABIKIR BADRI
Kuala Lumpur, Malaysia

CHAPTER ONE

Contemplation: A Modern Psychological Perspective

ISLAMIC CONTEMPLATION AND SECULAR PSYCHOLOGY

It may seem rather impertinent to discuss Islamic contemplation (*tafakkur*), which is one of the most exalted forms of worship in Islam, from the viewpoint of modern Western psychology – a secular and largely culture-bound discipline stocked with pseudo-knowledge disguised in the prestigious cloak of a science. However, since the Muslim laity and most students of psychology in the East are still dazzled by whatever is exported to them from the West, I realized the importance of starting the book with this chapter. I hope that this exposition will be helpful to Muslim lecturers who still teach Islamic ethics from Western psychoanalytically oriented textbooks on the psychology of religion. Though they claim to be Islamizing psychology, they may be unknowingly secularizing Islam! Since most of the readers of this book will probably not have studied modern Western psychology, I have intentionally simplified my exposition. Similarly, I felt that an in-depth critique of modern psychology from the Islamic perspective of contemplation as a form of worship would be too tedious for the general reader.

Contemplation as an Islamic form of worship may, at first, be viewed within the sphere of the recent interest of Western psychology in meditation procedures and their ability to bring about altered states of consciousness. However, although Islamic contemplation can achieve the relaxing benefits of meditation, as we shall see later, it differs from all the other forms of meditative procedures which are derived from Eastern religions in that its main objective is more cognitive and intellectual. In Islamic contemplation, altered states of consciousness are not an end in themselves, as the goal is a deeper insightful knowledge of God as the Creator and Sustainer of the universe. Consequently, an in-depth psychological discussion of Islamic contemplation would fall within the field of cognitive psychology, with special reference to the psychology of thinking.

The field of cognitive psychology, in its unrefined form, was the focus of the early schools of psychology before behaviorism became dominant. In those days, psychology was used mainly to study people's consciousness, their feelings, the content of their thoughts and the structure of their minds, attending to the question of learning only through these vistas. The behaviorist school introduced a totally new approach, where learning could be studied via stimuli and observable responses and became the basis of psychology; feelings, the components of the mind, and the process of thinking were considered questions that could not be observed directly, and the methods used to study them (such as introspection, and the observation and reporting of inner experiencing) were criticized as being vague and unreliable and could not be controlled by experimental procedures. Accordingly, the behaviorists who wanted psychology to become an exact experimental science, like physics and chemistry, restricted their work to phenomena that could be observed in the laboratory, and the responses that could be measured and controlled became the focus of their experimental and scientific concerns. On the other hand, the cognitive and emotional activities which take place inside the human being were considered something of a closed black box with contents that could not be observed, and for which, consequently, no time should be wasted in studying. Thus, the behaviorist vision of humans was that they were mere machines that, when exposed to specified stimuli, would react with responses which the researcher could control and predict. This approach automatically removed contemplation from being an area of psychological inquiry.

This effort to emulate physical and biological sciences by ignoring a person's spiritual and inner cognitive activities was unequivocally established by J. B. Watson, the founding father of behaviorism. He emphasized that people should be viewed as nothing more than animals; they are different from other animals only in the types of observable behavior that they perform. To be scientific, psychologists should therefore not allow themselves to study humans in any manner different from their work with animals. He writes that,

> [behaviorism] attempts to do one thing: to apply to the experimental study of man the same kind of procedure and the same language of description that many research men had found useful for so many years in the study of animals lower than man. We believed then, as we believe now, that man is an animal different from other animals only in the types of behavior he displays.
>
> The raw fact is that you, as a psychologist, if you are to remain scientific, must describe the behavior of man in no other terms than those you would use in describing the behavior of the ox you slaughter.[1]

Influenced by this constricted perspective, and encouraged by Ivan Pavlov's contributions to learning by conditioning, behaviorists went on to explain every human mental and psychological activity through the vision of stimulus-response connectionism. Even the process of thinking was explained in terms of a network of stimulus-response associations and considered as no more than a soliloquy.

The principal aim of this dehumanization of people was to mould psychology into a scientific cast. Another major objective was the secularization of Western societies and their emancipation from the grip of religion. In this connection, Watson clearly laments the fact that humans do not accept being classified as animals, and naïvely believe that God created them and that there is life after death. He states:

> Human beings do not want to class themselves with other animals. They are willing to admit that they are animals but 'something else in addition'. It is the 'something else' that causes the trouble. In this 'something else' is bound up everything that is classed as religion, the hereafter, morals, love of children, parents, country, and the like.[2]

From what has been said, it is obvious that behaviorism adamantly denies that humans have an innate good or evil nature, and that what they believe in is neither true nor false. Like a dry leaf on a windy day, their nature, values and beliefs are completely determined by environmental stimuli; there is no place in the behavioristic conception for any global ethical truths or moral standards. It also excludes any notion of human freedom of choice and any conscious moral or spiritual decision-making. Talking about contemplation and internal cognitive spiritual notions and feelings within the bounds of such a psychology would be inconceivable. The renowned British neurologist, John Eccles, endorses this criticism of behaviorism, saying that during the long dark night of the dominance of behaviorism,

> words like mind, consciousness, thoughts, purposes and beliefs were considered 'dirty' words unallowable in 'polite' philosophical discourse. Ironically, the most prominent philosophical obscenities were a new class of four-letter-words – mind, self, soul, will.[3]

Though other dominant perspectives and schools of psychology such as psychoanalysis and the biological perspective had, and still have, bitter disagreements with the behaviorists, they are in complete harmony when it comes to secularization and the downgrading of conscious thinking. Classical Freudian psychoanalysis, for instance, sees human behavior as fully determined by one's unconscious sexual and aggressive impulses, which means that people's conscious ideas, their contemplation, their judgments and their reasoning are but by-products of a deeper concealed mind of which they are unaware. Freud considered religion itself as an illusion and a mass obsessional neurosis!

Traditional neuropsychiatry, which is strongly based on an 'organicist' biological perspective, also depreciates the significance of conscious ideation, freedom of choice, and the unchanging spiritual moral standards of a human being. Biological determinism, in its exaggerated form, claims that anything, normal or abnormal, that people do is fully governed by their inherited genes, their nervous system, and inborn biochemistry. As one researcher describes it, "Behind any twisted idea or action, there is a twisted molecule in the brain." Theoretically, they believe that the way these inborn biological aspects interact with the environment is like a program in a computer's hard disk: if you happen to know all the particulars and variables you can predict accurately the future behavior of the person concerned. Consequently, they explain much of human ethical behavior, that religion has always considered to be the conscious choices of people and for which they should bear responsibility, in terms of irresistible biological determinism. For instance, a number of studies have tried to prove that promiscuity, homosexuality and lesbianism are deep-seated biologically programed urges, and that people should not, therefore, be condemned for following the instincts created by their genes.

If studying Islamic contemplation from the psychological point of view necessarily deals with the conscious inner cognitive thought and feelings of people, then these three dominant perspectives of Western psychology (behaviorism, Freudian psychoanalysis and neuropsychiatry) can offer little or no help. Indeed, two of these perspectives see humans as mechanical creatures dominated by external stimuli or biological and biochemical factors and, according to the third, our conscious thinking and feelings are simply a deception by our unconscious and ego defense mechanisms. It is not surprising, therefore, that these psychological schools and their artificial oversimplification of complex cognitive activities and feelings, in spite of securing respect for many years by providing scientific explanations of human behavior, have failed to provide satisfactory results. The optimism of fifty years ago has now dissipated, and the social and psychological problems of Western societies are probably the only variables that have surpassed economic inflation in their sharp increase. Their failure is not surprising since the psychology of humankind, with all its complex variables and spiritual aspects, could never be reduced to the chemical and physical data of laboratory experiments.

Precise disciplines such as physics and chemistry have made astonishing advances, not only because of the long period of their historic development – as some psychologists have us believe – but also, and more importantly, because of their purely material nature. These two disciplines built basic units of measurement and comprehensive theories to explain the behavior of matter and energy and their precise interaction. The two factors of matter and energy are fundamental because, without the concept of the atom and its components of protons and electrons, the experimental sciences could not have achieved so much. The same thing could be said about the cell as a basic unit in biology, or about the genes in the study of heredity.

In psychology, however, the complex nature of human behavior and its non-materialistic nature does not allow for such basic units or major underlying concepts. Any attempt to override this fact is inevitably met with failure and soon forgotten. We may take the concept of the conditioned reflex as an example to illustrate this difficulty, because it was regarded as one of the simplest concepts in psychology and was endorsed by many behaviorists.

What is a conditioned reflex? A hungry dog hears the sound of a bell and is immediately given some dried meat. The process is repeated until the dog salivates to the sound of the bell . This salivation to an artificial stimulus – the bell – is known as a conditioned reflex. Conditioning can also easily be applied to humans, such as when they learn to respond reflexively to a flashing light with a knee-jerk, or to the sound of a bell by blinking. Though this phenomenon was described by early Muslim scholars such as Ibn Sīnā and al-Ghazālī, it was first studied experimentally by Ivan Pavlov, the famous Russian physiologist.

Learning by conditioning can definitely explain some aspects of simple learning, but it cannot be taken as a serious unit in psychology because many areas of psychology are not based on such simple stimulus-response connections. For example, social psychology, humanistic psychology, perception, language-learning, and similar fields cannot be reduced to the simple stimulus-response paradigm of conditioning. Similarly, the deep and complex aspects of human behavior cannot be explained by conditioning laws. For example, how could one explain 'love' using stimuli and conditioned reflexes? The complex nature of this behavior has no room for such extreme fragmentation.

The same difficulties also prevented psychology from formulating a comprehensive theory like Einstein's theory of relativity in physics or Darwin's theory of evolution. Although recent scientific discoveries have now revealed certain flaws in the latter, it still serves as a general and comprehensive biological theory. Some schools and perspectives in modern psychology, such as psychoanalysis, Gestalt psychology and learning theory, tried to formulate an all-embracing theory, but none succeeded and their efforts simply became part of the history of Western psychology.[4]

These successive failures were evidently a logical outcome of the unreasonable efforts of modern psychologists to transform their discipline into an experimental science by neglecting people's inner feelings, consciousness, minds, and mental processes, as they had previously removed from them their souls and spiritual essence. This deformed approach was, from the start, strongly opposed by a number of clear-sighted scholars such as the British psychologist, Cyril Burt, who is often quoted to have said that psychology lost its soul, then its mind, and finally its consciousness, as if it were preparing itself for an ultimate demise.[5]

ISLAMIC CONTEMPLATION AND THE COGNITIVE REVOLUTION

One may not be as surprised to see the downfall of this distorted image of humankind in modern psychology as to realize that it took so long for Western psychologists to correct it. Psychology had to undergo a complete revolution to be able to reinstate its 'mind' and rediscover its inner conscious cognitive activities. This revolution is the contemporary cognitive revolution. Scholars began to show more interest in thinking and inner cognitive processes from about the middle of the twentieth century, but it took psychology several decades to recognize the superficiality of stimulus-response behaviorism and the unscientific distorted nature of the theories of psychoanalysis. This marked a return to the study of the internal mental activities used by people in analyzing and classifying information taken from their environment.

This new perspective in psychology is particularly important in that it shows the value of contemplation from both the scientific and religious points of view. Though this cognitive approach may be considered a return to the early stages of psychology, the methods used are much more advanced and depend on technologies especially devised to study human cognitive activities, on recent developments in neuroscience and, more importantly, on the computer revolution. Specialized research in these disciplines has clearly exposed the limited concept of a mechanical human being as adopted by behaviorism; this concept has been replaced with that of a human being as an 'information processor'.

When modern scholars compare people's thinking, inner cognitive and emotional processes and memory to a computer, they are describing the fact that they receive various stimuli from their environment, then code, classify and store them in their memory, to retrieve them when they need to solve new problems. In this simple analogy, receiving information from the environment corresponds to typing on the keyboard of a computer or feeding it in some other way; the central processing unit with its loaded software corresponds to the mind with its internal cognitive activity, like thinking and feeling; and the mental or behavioral responses that the person performs corresponds to what the computer shows on its monitor. The computer reacts differently to a specific letter struck on its keyboard according to the particular software program used and, similarly, people react differently to a specific stimuli to which they are subjected in their environment. Following the same logic, as we know exactly what kind of software is loaded in our computers, we should strive to know what 'software' is loaded in our minds as it is this 'software' which makes us think, feel and behave in the way we do. Thus the simple behavioristic conception of limiting research in psychology to stimuli that directly bring about responses has been equivocated.

It is interesting to note that although psychology and other social sciences continue to support the secular reductionistic view of human nature, they have changed their image of the human being according to progressive developments in technology. This computer model of the human being is clearly more realistic than the behaviorist model, since it tries to restore to modern psychology its 'mind' and 'consciousness', yet it obviously falls short of the true spiritual Islamic vision of humankind. Western psychology is still obsessed with an outdated tunnel-vision 'scientific' model. Furthermore, a paradigm shift in psychology, as in other social sciences, does not bring about a real revolution. Thomas Kuhn, the philosopher who popularized the concept of 'paradigm' and author of *The Structure of Scientific*

Revolutions, said that, "the more developed sciences had paradigms, but psychology didn't."[6]

This is obviously true, since in developed sciences a 'paradigm shift' results in a real revolution, where the new paradigm overthrows and replaces the old, just as Einstein's theories completely transformed Newtonian physics. In psychology and other social sciences, new paradigms – if we can call them so – generate much enthusiasm and attract many followers, but do not replace the old paradigms that continue to survive and sometimes flourish again a few years later. Thus, though the cognitive revolution is causing major changes in modern psychology, it cannot be considered a real rebellion against earlier concepts.

The real revolution in psychology will come when it regains its 'soul' and liberates itself from the constricted scientific and medical models for erecting an image of human nature. Indeed, the interaction of biological, psychological, and socio-cultural factors to produce a 'complex' of a thinking and behaving human being – as Western psychology still upholds – can never be as simple as the interaction of hydrogen, oxygen and carbon which occurs in photosynthesis when plants use solar energy to produce molecules of glucose from water and carbon dioxide.

However, even the revolution of cognitive psychology, which attempted to free the discipline from its constricted approach, still limits itself to this trio of psychological, biological and socio-cultural components of human behavior and mental processes. It has also ignored the spiritual component, despite increasing modern scientific evidence regarding its importance. By limiting itself to these three components because they are more easily defined compared with the spiritual aspect, or by simply rejecting the spiritual aspect because it emanates from a religious vision, modern psychology will remain ambiguous, inefficient and at a loss. It is like someone who anticipates the formation of glucose by the process of photosynthesis using the three elements of carbon, hydrogen and oxygen, but excluding solar energy simply because it is more sublime and less concrete. However, it must be stressed that even without the spiritual faith factor and despite the advance of knowledge, the study of these internal mental processes will always be a highly complex field where stimuli and their responses, causes and their effects interact in a manner which defies any sophisticated method of observation or measurement.

CONTEMPLATION AND THE BODY / MIND ENIGMA

The study of the internal psychological and mental world of the human being brings us face to face with one of man's most difficult questions: what is the connection between the body and the mind? The answer to this question is a medley of philosophical ideas, religious beliefs, psychological studies, biological and organic research findings about humankind in general, and the human brain and nervous system in particular. Discussing this issue in any detail is clearly beyond the bounds of this book. However, we cannot avoid a major controversy which is of relevance to our investigation on Islamic contemplation from the perspective of current psychobiological studies.

Though we know very little about the activities of the human brain, the materialists claim that the human being does not possess a 'mind', unless this word is used to mean the material 'brain' inside the skull. They also claim that what we call a 'thinking mind' is nothing but the reflections and 'translations' of the minute changes in the chemistry of the brain and its electrochemical nervous pulses – their justification being that people's thinking, and indeed their entire characters, change when the brain is damaged. This stand is obviously supported by behaviorists and other secular psychologists.

The opposing group affirms that there is a 'mind' that controls the brain and, ultimately, a person's behavior and thinking. Chief among this group is the neurologist, John Eccles, who won a Nobel Prize for his outstanding research on the nervous system. This scholar and the scientists who uphold his assertion affirm that their researches on the activity of the human brain and the nervous system can only be fully explained by the existence of a 'mind', a 'realizing soul', or what Eccles calls a 'self-conscious mind'.[7] They contend further that this non-material entity fully controls the nervous and behavioral activity of a human being. If the brain was the only entity governing the human cognitive processes and behavior, as materialists claim, no person would or could contest an action or decision taken by his brain. However, this is clearly not the case. Indeed, if, for example, a male volunteer is electrically stimulated in a certain part of the motor area of the cerebral cortex, he will respond with a jerking movement of his arm; if he is told not to move his arm, and the electrical stimulation of the brain is repeated, he will find his arm moving in spite of him; and if this process is repeated again, he may try to stop the movement of that arm with his other arm. This can be performed experimentally. Eccles would argue: if the brain was the only governing body, then the subject would not have negated what his brain had ordered; however, as this is not the case, then what caused the arm to move and what tried to stop it? Clearly, the brain moved it, and the mind tried to stop it.

Eccles and various other scholars often use the image of the relationship between a broadcasting station and a television set to explain the relationship between the mind and the brain. According to Eccles, the non-material, self-conscious, mind continuously scans, probes and controls the brain.[8] If the brain is damaged or if the person is unconscious, the mind will continue to do its job, but the outcome will depend on the quality and efficiency of reception by the brain. Similarly, if a television set develops a fault, the image it conveys will be disturbed or may disappear completely. Therefore, to say that the brain is the only element involved is a very naïve conception, just like the belief of a little child that the persons and images that appear on the television screen are actually inside the television set! This was the exact statement made by my four-year-old niece, Amina, when I told her that our guest, Hamid Umar al-Imam, was the distinguished shaykh who chanted the Qur'an every morning on Omdurman Radio. She said: "But Uncle, how can such a big man get inside our small radio?"

In the impressive volume, *The Self and Its Brain*, that Eccles wrote with the renowned philosopher Karl Popper, the author comes very close to agreeing with the religious belief about the immortality of the soul. As an open-minded scientist, convinced by his research on the existence of a self-conscious mind, he asks himself: what happens to this mind after death?

> Finally, of course we come to the ultimate picture, what happens in death? Then all cerebral activity ceases permanently. The self-conscious mind that has had an autonomous existence in a sense…now finds that the brain it had scanned and probed and controlled so efficiently and effectively through a long life is no longer giving any messages at all. What happens then is the ultimate question.[9]

As Eccles has asserted, what takes place after the death of the brain is the ultimate question that will continue to haunt scholars as well as lay people. It will forever mystify us because God decreed that knowledge about the true nature of the soul or spirit, how it interacts with the body and what happens to it after death, was to be a strictly guarded secret curtailed from us in this world. Indeed, knowing what happens after death would necessarily reveal the secret of our soul and spirit and, if this happened, then the whole religious conviction of this life as a testing place would be invalidated. When asked about the spirit, Prophet Muhammad received the following revelation: "They ask you about the spirit. Say, 'The spirit is of the command of my Lord. It is only a little knowledge about it that is communicated to you'" (17:85). Thus, knowledge of the true nature of the spirit is unattainable. And for this reason, Islam urges the Muslim worshipper to concentrate his contemplative efforts on the attainable. The complete answer to this question will therefore remain unresolved.

Some scholars may believe that trying to tackle this problem from the purely biological aspect may be easier and 'scientifically' more straightforward than the more intangible philosophical, religious or psychological aspects. However, the truth of the matter is that the biological perspective is not less complicated; in fact, it could be even more complicated since an in-depth investigation in biology and physics can often end up in philosophy and spirituality. In his valuable book, *The Psychobiology of the Mind*, W. Uttal says that all the modern research and discoveries about the workings of the human brain have not brought us any closer to solving the problem of the relation between body and mind.[10] In fact, they have simply added new questions; the basic questions asked in the days of Aristotle, more than 2,000 years ago, are still waiting for satisfactory answers.

Another complication raised by modern biological research about the relation between body and mind is the role of the human heart in influencing the brain and shaping neural behavior. According to Joseph Pearce in his thought-provoking book, *Evolution's End*, the human heart is much more than a pumping station; it is the organ that alerts the brain to carry out appropriate responses. Neuro-transmitters, which play an important role in the functioning of the brain, have been found in the heart. He says: "Actions in the heart precede the actions of both body and brain...We know now that the heart...controls and governs the brain action through hormonal, transmitter, and possibly finer quantum-energies of communication."[11]

If what Pearce says is true, then artificial plastic hearts will not be able to do what a real or transplanted heart can do. It would also mean that a person who receives a transplanted heart will somehow behave in ways similar to that of the donor. And finally, there must be some scientific evidence for the proposed non-localized influence or 'remote control' of the heart over the brain and body.

Concerning the first issue, Pearce relies on the authority of the heart surgeon who pioneered in heart transplantation, Christian Barnard, who said: "We must give up the idea of an artificial heart, since we have found the organ to be far more than just a pumping station."[12]

As for the second point, Pearce confirms that though the heart is governed by a 'higher' order of energy (or a 'soul' in Islamic belief), the behavior of "people getting heart-transplants often dramatically reflect certain behaviours of the late donors."[13] And regarding the possibility of non-localization, he refers the reader to convincing experiments in which two cells taken from the heart are observed through a microscope. In the first experiment in which they are isolated from one another, they simply fibrillate until they die. However, when similar cells are brought near to each other, they synchronize and beat in unison:

> They don't have to touch; they communicate across a spatial barrier...Our heart, made up of many billions of such cells operating in unison, is under the guidance of a higher, non-localised intelligence...

> So we have both a physical heart and a higher 'universal heart' and our access to the latter is...dramatically contingent on the...former.[14]

According to Pearce, when we are in deep spiritual contemplation, we are drawing from our spiritual universal heart, which influences our physical heart, that communicates with our brain and influences our cognitive activities. This, in some respects, is very similar to the views of Abū Ḥāmid al-Ghazālī in his monumental work *Iḥyā' ʿUlūm al-Dīn* (The Revival of the Religious Sciences) in which he clearly states that although the spiritual heart (*qalb*), which is the controlling centre of the soul, is different from the physical human heart, its functioning is related and directed by it. We can thus see how a biological discourse develops into a religious dialogue.[15]

However, as Uttal argues, despite all the recent achievements in science and technology, we are still ignorant of the way the nervous system provides human beings with their consciousness and their sense of being, which are their dearest possessions. This, I believe, is really a matter for contemplation and meditation about the creation and about the essence of contemplation itself, and in all its psychological, spiritual and behavioral aspects. These questions are expressed succinctly by the Sudanese poet, Yūsuf Bashīr al-Tijānī, who addresses the mind in his poem 'Prophets of Truth':

> Lord, grant me Your grace, how moulded
> Your Hand the hidden, mysterious talisman
> Called mind, by You in eternity?
> Who planned and directed life?
> Lord, grant me Your grace: this mind,
> Who stopped it from being visible to us?
> Its being, hidden from itself, has it
> Become accidence in time, or remained an essence?
> O mind, O delusion of the mind,
> Do you not have a better claim to yourself?
> O powers that demolish and build up life,
> And can turn the world into ashes and dust.[16]

LANGUAGE: THE MAIN VEHICLE OF CONTEMPLATION

Despite the complexity of this problem, research in cognitive psychology has become familiar with many secrets of human internal intellectual and mental activities and their precise relation with language. With the help of modern computer scientists, it has been possible to set up simplified programs to clarify some of the methods followed by the human mind in classifying information. It has been found, for instance, that language is not only a human being's means of address and communication, but also the basic system used in thinking. Without the laws that control the way in which tangible and abstract meanings are conveyed through word symbols, human beings cannot develop abstract concepts. They cannot use either their sensory perception or their ability to imagine and remember in dealing with various types of experiences they underwent in the past, so that they can relate them to the present and deduce from them possible solutions to problems they are facing. Thinking, in fact, is using such symbols through cognitive processes.

Some researchers, like Whorf who formulated the 'linguistic relativity' hypothesis, consider the characteristics of the language spoken by a certain group of people to be the factor that denoted how they think and how they visualize the realities they live. The structure and other aspects of language are therefore considered to be basic factors in the way a given society visualizes the world.

Let us take a closer look at this idea of the importance of language. If it were wholly or even partly true, it would be most appropriate for us to consider the characteristics of the Arabic language, its impact on the Arabs and the reasons for the divine choice of this language as the means to reveal the Qur'an and convey the message of Islam to the whole of humanity. God says in the Qur'an: "We have, without doubt, sent down the Message; and we will assuredly guard it" (15:9). This means that He guards Revelation and, consequently, also the Arabic language. In this connection, the Egyptian scholar, ʿAbbās Maḥmūd al-ʿAqqād, discusses some aspects of the Arabic language: its vocabulary, phonetic and phonemic aspects:

> The human speech system is a superb musical instrument which no ancient or modern nation has used as perfectly as the Arab nation, as they have used the entire phonetic range in the distribution of its alphabet. Therefore, it is these qualities of the Arabic language that made Arabic poetry a perfect art, independent of other arts.[17]

According to al-ʿAqqād, these qualities are not found in any other language, for "Arabic eloquence has taken the human speech organs to the highest point ever reached by man in expressing himself by letters and words."[18]

In *Al-Fuṣḥā: Lughat al-Qur'ān* (Classical Arabic: The Language of the Qur'an), Anwar al-Jundī mentions the qualities of the Arabic language and its importance in propagating Islam:

> It is most astonishing to see this robust language (Arabic) growing and reaching a stage of perfection in the midst of the desert, and in a nation of nomads. The language has superseded other languages by its wealth of vocabulary, precise meanings and perfect structure. This language was unknown to other nations. But when it came to be known, it appeared to us in such perfection that it hardly underwent any change ever since. Of the stages of life, that language had neither childhood nor old age. We hardly know anything about that language beyond its unmatched conquests and victories. We cannot find any similar language that appeared to scholars so complete, and without gradation, keeping a structure so pure and flawless. The spread of the Arabic language covered the largest areas and remotest countries.[19]

FROM COGNITIVE ACTIVITY TO ESTABLISHED NORMAL AND ABNORMAL HABITS

After this digression about the importance of language as a basic system for thinking, we turn to the research of cognitive psychologists and computer scientists in their attempts to understand human internal cognitive activities. Both are concerned with the study of the human capacity to analyze, classify and store information in the memory so as to retrieve it when needed. They have conducted many detailed studies to examine the processes used by a human being in thinking and problem-solving then, using this data, they have established various programs imitating human cognitive activity. Some have even created a program that tries to imitate the way of thinking of neurotics and psychotics in their adjustment to their environment. These studies have clarified many aspects that the behaviorists had chosen to ignore because they felt it was impossible to identify its contents, and have produced many theories and explanations that challenge the naïve concept of stimulus-response psychology. These studies have also opened a window for the Muslim psychologist to learn more about the importance of contemplation and worship, and the concomitant internal mental-cognitive activity associated with them. Psychotherapists and personality psychologists have made use of these cognitive studies that disclose human internal thinking and feelings and examine the formation of observable normal and abnormal human behavior.

As we have mentioned earlier, the behaviorists emphasize the role of the environment as the only influence responsible for the development of the human personality and normal and abnormal human behavior. This is to say, they believe that environmental stimuli directly lead to the behavioral responses. The cognitive psychologists, on the other hand, are more concerned with the meanings produced by these experiences. They claim that an experience does not automatically provoke a response, except in the case of reflexes – like pulling the hand away when it touches a hot surface. Complex responses that influence people's ideas, beliefs, voluntary decisions and observable complex behavior come from previous conceptualizations, emotions and experiences which give meaning to subsequent environmental stimuli. In other words, it is what people think about that affects their beliefs, feelings and consequent behavior. If their thinking is centered on the creation and bounties of the Almighty, their faith will increase and their deeds and behavior will improve; if it is centered on their pleasures and desires, they will be distracted from their religion and their behavior will degenerate; and if their thinking is about their fears, frustrations, failures and consequent pessimism, they will be afflicted with reactive depression and other psychological disorders. Consequently, cognitive psychologists concentrate their therapy on changing patients' conscious thinking as it is the activity that usually precedes the feelings and emotional responses of normal and neurotic people. In other words, they try to change the 'software' used by their minds, as it is the program they use which gives meaning to what they experience. This internal cognitive activity (automatic thoughts) may be so rapid and spontaneous that the individual does not notice it except after thorough analysis and training.

This research has shown that every intentional action performed by the individual is preceded by an internal cognitive activity. They have also proved that the human mind never stops this cognitive activity at any moment of the day or night, whether the individual is aware of it or not. A classic illustration of this is when someone is unable to find a solution to a problem, so puts it aside and moves on to a different activity; then, suddenly, the solution comes to mind without a conscious effort by that person or any expectation. A famous example of this is Archimedes' sudden discovery of the fluid displacement law. Similarly, someone who fails to remember a name or a word will suddenly remember it some time later.

Therefore, it is the internal cognitive activity of a human being, whether conscious or unconscious, that directs observable human behavior. This conclusion was reached by cognitive psychologists after long years of research, overstepping all the psychological schools that tried to confine complex human general behavior into simplistic theories. Furthermore, this cognitive perspective clearly supports what Islam had already established: that contemplation, as an internal thought process, is the backbone of faith which is the source of every good deed.

In addition to this discovery that every action begins with an internal cognitive activity – be it a notion, a memory, an image, a perception, or an emotion – it has also been shown that when this cognitive activity gains strength, it can become a motive or an incentive for action; and if the individual performs this motivated action repeatedly, then these internal ideas can easily and spontaneously make it become a rooted habit. This habit is not necessarily a skill; it can be an emotion, a spiritual feeling, or an attitude. So, if the cognitive therapist wishes to treat a patient who suffers from an emotional or other kind of habit, he must strive to change the internal thinking that causes this behavior. If the habit is fear of social situations, for instance, the therapist has to identify the negative thinking that causes the patient to respond with this social fear. For example, if the patient imagines that he would look silly if he were to talk or introduce himself to strangers, or if he were to deliver a speech before a group of acquaintainces, the therapist can then help the patient change these negative thoughts by showing that they are irrational, have no basis in reality, and that the patient's feelings blindly followed his pessimistic thinking until he was wrongly convinced by them to the extent that they took control of his behavior. When these internal notions are changed, the behavior will change accordingly.

This kind of therapy can also be performed by stimulating responses that are contrary to the negative ideas, fancies, and internal emotions that cause the habit. In the case of fear of social situations, for instance, the therapist can stimulate in the patient a relaxing feeling of security and psychological comfort, while at the same time exposing him to increasingly difficult social situations (whether real or imaginary).

On the other hand, if the negative habit causes the patient some pleasure and psychological comfort, such as gambling, drinking alcohol or performing certain deviant sexual behavior, the treatment by countermeasures leads the therapist to stimulate a sense of pain, psychological stress and fear in the patient when he repeats that particular negative habit. In this type of aversion therapy, an alcoholic or drug addict, for instance, is given injections of a chemical material that will cause him to have nausea and headaches when he drinks alcohol; he may even be exposed to painful but harmless electric shocks. This 'reward and punishment' therapy is known as 'reciprocal inhibition' and is one of the most successful techniques of modern behavioral therapy. Though devised by behaviorists, the cognitive therapists have developed it by relating it to the thinking and the conscious feelings of the patient. This marriage of aspects of behavior modification with the recent developments in cognitive therapy is the latest and most successful innovation in psychological therapy.

Cognitive psychology, therefore, affirms that people's conscious thinking and inner dialogues influence their feelings and emotions, and form their attitudes and beliefs – in short, they can even shape their values and vision of life. If the discussion is transferred from the cognitive therapy of the emotionally disturbed to the cognitive activity of normal Muslims, one can clearly see the great influence of the cognitive processes involved in contemplation in remodeling the very psyche of individuals. Furthermore, if the spritual/faith factor is added – a factor which is a powerful cognitive force totally excluded by modern psychology – one can imagine the momentous change that Islamic contemplation can achieve in purifying the souls and elevating the status of the worshippers. Through contemplation, Muslims can refine their own internal 'reward and punishment' psychospiritual strategies in their spiritual development; they do not need a worldly reward or an electric shock to change their unwanted habits and replace them with more worthy ones. By devoting their internal cognitive and spiritual aspirations to the contemplation of God's majesty and perfection in contrast to their laxity and unworthy behavior, they will certainly develop the sentiment of love of God and the refined feelings of contentment, happiness and tranquillity. This will be discussed in more detail in the following chapter.

CHAPTER TWO

Contemplation: The Works of Early Muslim Scholars

In the previous chapter the latest achievements of psychology in the field of human thinking and cognitive activities have been summarized and simplified to show the significance of contemplation, as a form of worship, in directing the behavior of Muslims and enhancing their faith. Indeed, once it is realized that internal thinking, emotions, perceptions, imagination and ideas all influence the formation of an individual's behavior – his tendencies, beliefs, conscious and unconscious activities, good and bad habits – it is possible to see why the Qur'an and the Sunnah are so concerned with meditation and the contemplation of the creation of the heavens and the earth, as they fill the heart and mind with the majesty of the Creator and the nobility of His attributes. Ibn Qayyim al-Jawziyyah stated in his notable work, *Miftāḥ Dār al-Saʿādah* (The Key to the House of Bliss): "Deep thought (contemplation)...is the beginning of and the key to all good...it is the best function of the heart and the most useful to it."[1]

It took Western psychology more than seven decades to return to the 'common sense' recognition of the influence of thinking and cognitive processes in shaping human beliefs, attitudes and external behavior. These achievements were not unknown to the early scholars of Islam. Indeed, the cognitive principles and practices which have only recently impressed modern Western psychology were already known, centuries ago, by scholars such as Ibn Qayyim al-Jawziyyah (also known as Ibn al-Qayyim), al-Balkhī, al-Ghazālī, Miskawayh, and many others. In his masterpiece, *Maṣāliḥ al-Abdān wa al-Anfus* (The Sustenance of the Body and the Soul), Abū Zayd al-Balkhī showed the influence of contemplation and inner thought on health – a discovery that was only developed more than ten centuries after his death. He even suggested that just as a healthy person keeps some drugs and first-aid medicines at hand for unexpected physical emergencies, he should also contemplate and keep healthy thoughts and feelings in his mind for unexpected emotional outbursts.[2]

Other early Muslim scholars mentioned the importance of notions, reflections and ideas that cross the mind and can grow to become drives and incentives that are carried out in real life, and, when repeated, become habits. They also referred to the unceasing internal cognitive activity of human beings – an activity, they assert, that is never interrupted, whether in a person's waking or sleeping hours. These scholars gave genuine advice to those who wanted to perform good deeds, urging them to watch their notions and internal ideas, to remember God constantly, and to meditate on and contemplate the creation of the heavens and the earth. They also said that a person should try to change harmful notions and internal ideas before they become desires and drives, because changing a drive or motive is easier than stopping a consequent action, and removing an action is easier than trying to uproot it after it has become a habit. They stated further, in the words of modern behavior therapists, that treating a habit should be done by training the individual to do its opposite. All this was recorded by Ibn al-Qayyim in *Al-Fawā'id* (The Spiritual Benefits), and in such detail that it sounded as if he were familiar with the latest achievements of modern cognitive psychology.

In this work, Ibn al-Qayyim explicitly says that anything a person does begins as an inner thought, a concealed speech or an internal dialogue, for which he uses the Arabic word, *khawāṭir*. The word *khawāṭir* is the plural of *khaṭirah,* meaning a fast, inner, concealed reflection, notion or subvocal thought, which may come fleetingly. Modern cognitive psychologists can compare this with the idea of 'automatic thoughts' which the cognitive therapist Aaron Beck claims to have discovered in the 1970s! In his classic book, *Cognitive Therapy and the Emotional Disorders*, he devotes six pages to a section titled 'The discovery of automatic thoughts' to describe how he arrived at this 'discovery'.[3]

After describing this cognitive conception, Ibn al-Qayyim details the exact process by which fleeting thoughts, particularly negative ones, develop into human actions and observable behavior. He warns that a lustful, sinful, or emotionally harmful *khaṭirah*, if accepted and not checked by the person concerned, can develop into a strong emotion or lust (*shahwah*). If this emotion is entertained or given credence, it may generate so much cognitive strength that it develops into a drive or an impulse for action. And if this impulsive drive or emotional motivation is not neutralized by its opposite emotion or resisting drive, it will be acted out in reality as external behavior. Furthermore, if this behavior is not resisted, it will be repeated so often that it becomes a habit. In this respect, Ibn al-Qayyim believed that emotional, physical and cognitive habits followed the same pattern – a belief which is strikingly similar to the modern approach of cognitive psychologists. He also details a different route in his *Al-Fawā'id*, whereby fleeting reflections become real actions and established attitudes:

> You should know that the beginning of any voluntary act is *khawāṭir* and *wasāwis* [*wasāwis* is the plural of *waswasah* which means concealed whisper. It is used in the Qur'an to describe the inner temptation of Satan: *yuwaswisu fī ṣudūri al-nās*]. These *khawāṭir* and *wasāwis* lead to conscious thinking. Next, thinking will be transferred to or stored in the memory and the memory will transform it into a volition and a motive which will be acted out in real life as an action. Repeating the action leads to a strong habit. So eliminating an emotional or lustful habit is easier at an early stage before it gains strength.[4]

Thus, he advises the Muslim to lead a happy and righteous life by fighting the negative *khawāṭir* and *wasāwis* of inner fleeting thoughts before they become an emotion or an impulse. Indeed, it is easier to check inner fleeting thoughts than to fight an impulse, as it is easier to resist an impulse with an opposing motive than to change the behavior after it is actually performed, and easier to refrain from an action performed only once or a few times than waiting until it has become a habit.

In addition, Ibn al-Qayyim gives a good description of inner cognitive activity, and warns his readers that God has not given humankind the ability to totally eradicate fleeting thoughts and reflections, for they are as irresistible as breathing. However, a wise person, who has strong faith in God, can accept the good *khawāṭir* and avoid the bad and potentially harmful ones. God, he states, has created the human mind in a way very similar to a rotating millstone which never stops, day or night, but grinds continually, and always needs something to grind. Some people, who feed their minds with good thoughts and spiritual contemplation, are like those who put corn and wheat in their mills: they produce good flour. However, the millstones of most people grind dirt and stones. When the time for making bread comes (in the hereafter), each group will know what their mills have been grinding!

Ibn al-Qayyim then states that actions and deeds can only be sound when their internal and contemplative notions originate from a warm spiritual relationship with God. He writes:

> These [cognitive] stages are sound when notions and ideas are sound, and they are depraved with the depravity of those notions and ideas. They are sound in so far that they look up towards their Lord and God, aspiring to Him and striving for His pleasure. The Almighty is the source of all soundness and guidance. His grace is the source of righteousness, and His protection of His servant is the fount of safety. When the servant of the Almighty turns away and evades the Lord, he strays onto the way of perdition.[5]

This discourse reads like a summary of modern behavioral cognitive therapy in a modern textbook of psychology, with the addition of the spiritual faith dimension which is lacking in modern secular psychology. Much of this literature by early Muslim scholars is based on knowledge acquired from the Qur'an and the Sunnah, which is moulded into useful psychological principles.

As previously explained, modern behavioral and cognitive therapy has established the fact that the most successful treatment of psychological and emotional disorders is to encourage patients to evoke thoughts and feelings of tranquillity and gradually help them change their undesirable habits, as is done in reciprocal inhibition – a method of therapy which Ibn al-Qayyim had also mentioned on several occasions many centuries ago. As a matter of fact, this successful behavioral and cognitive therapy, which depends on in-depth thought and imagination on the part of the patients, also depends on their ability to contemplate. This is particularly apparent in one of the most successful modern treatments, known as systematic desensitization, in which patients are instructed to relax and imagine themselves in a place of beautiful scenery like a beach or an area of greenery with flowing streams. While in this pleasing tranquil meditation, they are instructed to imagine the situations that had caused their emotional troubles. This is repeated until the tranquil feelings psychologically 'overpower' the evoked anxiety. In fact, it may be more conveniently termed 'contemplation therapy' instead of systematic desensitization.

Al-Ghazālī contributed much to the theoretical aspects of contemplation therapies, but he also turned to their practical aspects by giving several realistic examples. In *Iḥyā' ʿUlūm al-Dīn,* he says that the Muslim who wants to adhere to good behavior has first to change his ideas about himself and imagine himself in the desired condition. Then he must gradually assume those good manners until they become part of him. Al-Ghazālī affirms that interaction between the psychocognitive aspect and practical behavior is inevitable. Once the individual behaves in a certain manner, even if he feigns what he does, the effect of that behavior will reflect on his thinking and emotions; and when his thinking and feelings change, his observable behavior and countenance will also change. He describes this process as follows:

> Good manners can be acquired by practice: by feigning or assuming the actions issuing from those manners at first until they eventually become part of one's nature. This is one of the wonders of the relation between the heart and the organs – I mean the soul and the body. Every quality that appears in the heart will have its influence flowing to the organs so they act only in accordance with that quality. Similarly, the effect of every action that issues from the organs may reach the heart. And this continues in a circular system.[6]

He also mentions the therapeutic value of combining the treatment that uses opposing stimulation with a gradual approach based on internal cognition. He writes, as if he were summarizing the latest achievements of modern cognitive behavioral therapy, using a few clear words and precise, tangible examples to compare the soma with the psyche:

> Since the malady that changes the health of the body and causes illness can only be treated with its opposite, like treating heat with cold, and cold with heat, so vice, which is a malady of the heart, is treated with its opposite. The malady of ignorance is treated with learning, that of avarice with generosity, pride with humility, greed with abstinence, and all by assuming the contrary...
>
> A curious aspect of this exercise is noticeable when the disciple is not willing to give up a serious offence or reprehensible wrongdoing by directly assuming its opposite. Then his shaykh [master] should lead him from that greatly undesirable habit to another one, less undesirable. This is like someone who washes the bloodstain off his shirt with urine, then washes the urine off with water, when water cannot wash off blood.[7]

He then quotes an example of a man who used to complain of a hot temper and outbursts of anger: he began to train himself gradually to be more patient, and to change his reactions and emotions by inner thought and contemplation combined with actual practice in life situations. He went as far as: "...paying a man to insult him in front of people, and he would try to be patient and control his anger by spiritually sedating himself with remembrance and contemplation, until patience was part of his nature and he became proverbial in that respect."[8]

This example shows that contemplation and concomitant remembrance of God are the backbone for the positive changes Muslims can accomplish in themselves, and that without these changes, the modification of habits and behavior would not be feasible. That is why al-Ghazālī insists in *Al-Ḥikmah fī Makhlūqāt Allāh* (The Wisdom Behind God's Creation) that contemplation is the key to every good deed, because it qualifies all cognitive actions of the believer with the remembrance of the Almighty and the recognition of His favors and grace. He says:

> The way to a cognizance of God is to glorify Him in His creation, to contemplate His wonderful works, to understand the wisdom in His various inventions...It is the means to strengthen certainty and happiness, and in this course is seen the difference in the levels of the pious...The Almighty created the minds and perfected them with revelation, ordering men with such minds to think of His creatures, to contemplate and learn a lesson from what wonders He has entrusted in His creation.[9]

Clearly, such contemplation covers the intellectual, emotional, temperamental and perceptive aspects of believers – that is, all their psychological, cognitive, and spiritual actions. It is difficult to imagine those who remember God but do not contemplate His creation, or those who contemplate God's creation but do not remember Him. This reminds us of the famous statement by al-Ḥasan al-Baṣrī: "Men of knowledge have been resorting to thought with the remembrance of God (dhikr), and to the remembrance of God with thought, imploring the hearts to speak, until the hearts responded with wisdom."[10]

When people contemplate, it becomes a sacred and wholesome part of their nature: their hearts become submissive and they respond to every agitation in their environment with gentle emotions which control their intellectual activity. It was once said to a worshipper, "You contemplate for long hours." He replied: "Contemplation is the core of the mind." Sufyan al-Thawrī often quoted these lines of poetry:

> When a man is used to contemplation,
> He will learn a lesson from everything.[11]

Since the origin of every action is a cognitive, emotional, or intellectual mental activity, those who are given to long periods of contemplation will perform their acts of worship and obedience quite easily. Referring to this fact, al-Ghazālī writes in *Iḥyā' ʿUlūm al-Dīn* about the value of knowledge and inner thought in contemplation in the clearest and most eloquent way:

> When knowledge enters the heart, the state of the heart changes. When this changes, the functions of the organs change. Functions follow the state of the heart, and this follows knowledge. And knowledge follows thought. Thought, then, is the beginning and the key to all good. This will show you the virtue of contemplation, and that it supersedes remembrance, since the thought includes remembrance and more.[12]

While internal cognitive activity is the key to every good and proper action, it is also the source of all disobedience, whether implied or overt. A meditative heart, which contemplates the grace of God and is mindful of the hereafter, can easily detect the evil notions that pass through the mind as a result of the great sensitivity that the mind has acquired from long contemplation and continued remembrance. As soon as an evil notion passes through the mind, good sense detects it, confines it, and defuses its effect, just as a sound immune system in the body detects the intrusion of germs and antigens, which it then besieges and destroys with specialized cells and antibodies. The psyche or soul of those who are constantly contemplating the grace of God is like a protected fortress: whenever evil notions try to enter, the acute perception acquired through contemplation and remembrance quickly attacks and destroys them. The Qur'an states: "Those who fear God, when an evil thought from Satan assaults them, bring God to mind, and lo! They see clearly"(7:201).

Contemplation, then, makes use of all the cognitive activities employed by a human being in the thinking processes. However, it differs from secular in-depth thinking in that its visions and concepts go beyond this world of the here and now to encounter the infinite dimensions of the hereafter; its object goes from the creation to the Creator. While everyday thinking may be limited to the solving of worldly problems, and may be free from sentiments, passions and emotions, contemplation, by virtue of its crossing the worldly barriers and the limitations of matter into the everlasting freedom of the spirit, is capable of motivating all the internal and external psychospiritual reservoirs of the believers. Those believers who are absorbed in deep Islamic contemplation perceive the things they are contemplating in terms of their previous experiences, as well as through the symbols and expressions they acquired from their use of language, and their imagination of what they used to be and what they could become in the future. They then vitalize the whole combination of different thoughts and visions with a fearful love of the Almighty. Thus, although Islamic contemplation may be regarded as a mixture of thought, cognition, imagination, sentiments, emotions and, above all, spirituality, the result is a completely new experience different from the elements of which it is composed.

This process can be related to the analogy of photosynthesis described above. As photosynthesis in plants cannot be accomplished without the elements of carbon, oxygen and hydrogen, Islamic contemplation cannot be achieved without psychological 'ingredients' such as thought, imagination and feelings. Sunlight shines on green leaves with an energy that completely transforms the clear gas, carbon dioxide and transparent water into a new substance, glucose, that has no resemblance to either hydrogen, oxygen or black carbon. Similarly, radiating spirituality illuminates the soul and metamorphoses the internal cognitive processes into a new exalted state.

This concept brings to mind al-Ghazālī's affirmation that Islamic contemplation "presents two data to the heart in order to motivate a third one." He says:

> He who inclines to the transient world and prefers the present life, and would like to know whether the hereafter is to be preferred to the transient world, has to know, firstly, that the permanent is preferable; and secondly, that the hereafter is permanent. Out of these two data he will obtain a third one, which is that the hereafter is preferable. To realize that the hereafter is preferable to the transient is only possible by means of the former two data.[13]

Al-Ghazālī believes that the growth of data can only be achieved by this coupling process because, according to him, the knowledge of data is a product of former knowledge. He affirms that if the contemplative believer is able to organize his knowledge in a certain manner, it will increase indefinitely, and nothing will stop it except the obstacles of life or death. In this way, al-Ghazālī shows the difference between material thinking and contemplation: man will be deprived of the knowledge that comes from contemplation if he does not have the basic data to help him in the process of contemplation. Indeed, an ignorant Bedouin may not be able to usefully contemplate the subject of the electrons and protons that form the atom; and similarly, those who deny God cannot contemplate the Divine Being, even if they are specialists in physics. Al-Ghazālī says:

> Most people cannot increase their knowledge for they do not have the capital, which is the basic data for investment in knowledge. This is like someone who has no commodity and therefore cannot make a profit. Or, he may have the commodity, but has no experience in business. He may even have the data, which are the capital of knowledge, but he does not know how to use the data to bring about the coupling that leads to the production of the profit.[14]

Islamic contemplation passes through three interconnected stages, leading to the fourth and final stage which I call the stage of 'spiritual cognition' (*shuhūd*). The first stage is when knowledge of the contemplated object comes through direct sensory perception – via sight, hearing, touch, smell and taste – or indirectly, as in the case of imagination. Such information can be purely mental and often has no relation to emotional or sentimental aspects.

The second stage of contemplation starts when a person takes a closer look at these data, inspecting their aesthetic aspects and particular qualities. It is a shift from mere perception to a state of wonder at the beauty, excellence, vastness of structure, and miraculous appearance of the perceived object. It is a stage of fine appreciation, delicate feelings and powerful passion.

The third stage is when the meditator crosses the boundary between the created object of contemplation and its Creator. He or she is then carried away by feelings of submission to and appreciation of the One Who brought the appreciated object of contemplation, as well as everything else in this universe, into being because of the meditator's realization that there is nothing in existence save God and what He has originated.

When this refined meditation is repeated and reinforced with continual remembrance of the Almighty, it leads the worshipper to the fourth stage: spiritual cognition. Here, the spiritual feelings associated with deep contemplation become part of the worshipper's nature, and make him or her more loving toward and fearful of God and His sublime Attributes. These feelings, continually experienced, are beyond verbal description.

Observing creation is only a primitive stage that can be enjoyed by believers and unbelievers alike. Similarly, the second stage, that of appreciating the beauty of form and structure, can touch the hearts of both believers and unbelievers. However, the third stage, which relates this aesthetic appreciation of the universe to the Almighty Creator, can only be achieved by believers. As for the believers who reach the fourth stage, they are in such deep veneration and remembrance of God that they can no longer look at God's creation in a detached manner; they see nothing but precision, mercy, beauty and wisdom in the structure of the world, and become ever more awestricken and appreciative of the glory of the Lord. This modern perception of Islamic contemplation can be related to the words of al-Ḥasan al-Baṣrī, quoted above: "Men of knowledge have been resorting to thought with the remembrance of God, and to the remembrance of God with thought, imploring the hearts to speak until the hearts responded with wisdom."[15]

From the perspective of learning and habit-formation, it can be said that believers who regularly contemplate will reach the fourth stage, because meditation, strengthened with constant remembrance, becomes a deep-rooted spiritual habit. This kind of level of thinking could only occur otherwise as a result of impressive experiences or rare events that totally disturb their environment, such as an earthquake or the death of a powerful revered person. For contemplative believers, the period of contemplation will gradually expand until they spend a greater part of the day and night in this elevated kind of meditation. Familiar objects, which they used to pass by without noticing, become a source of deep thought and a pretext for greater veneration of and meditation on the grace of God – thus everything in their environment becomes a motivation for thought and a drive for remembrance.

The stage of insightful cognition which the meditative believers then reach is a subject of lengthy discussion by many scholars. For example, Ibn al-Qayyim describes in *Madārij al-Sālikīn* (The Path of Seekers), the Muslim who reaches the stage of spiritual cognition:

> The gate to witnessing the greatness of God and the scene of sovereignty are opened before him...He sees that all the cosmic changes and the affairs of existence are in the hands of the Almighty alone. Then he observes the signs of the Holder of good and evil, creation and livelihood, resurrection and death...Then, if his eye notices any part of the creation, it will lead him to his Creator and to the contemplation of His Attributes of perfection and majesty.[16]

Ibn Taymiyyah terms this stage of contemplation the 'true cognition', when the contemplative believer witnesses

> all creation performing the orders of God, directed by His will, responsive and submissive to Him...What the contemplative believers thus witness will enhance and enlarge what their hearts hold of religious loyalty...not forgetting to differentiate the Eternal from the expirable, the Creator from His creation, and His oneness and independence from His creation.[17]

In fact, the believers who reach the second stage and appreciate the beauty of creation, its magnitude and precision, will be inevitably drawn closer toward the Maker and Regulator, and will begin to feel their own insignificance and helplessness in comparison with all His signs in the heavens and on the earth. This vast universe is indeed nothing but a place of worship to which only believers can have access, when their souls are refined, their hearts are submissive, and they are able to listen to and witness the truth.

The believers' bewilderment at the precision, beauty and magnitude of creation, and their realization of their comparative physical and psychological meagerness, are feelings that the Creator implanted in human beings so that they could look to the heavens and the earth for guidance toward their Lord, and so that they would worship Him with awe and deep veneration. Failing this recognition, they go astray into unbelief and paganism, and use their inborn nature in an adverse manner. Indeed, this bewilderment has led the followers of pagan religions throughout history to exaggerate the size, beauty and design of their temples, embellishing them with statues, paintings and inspiring music. We can mention, for instance, the Pantheon in Athens; or the Temple of Jupiter at Baalbek in Lebanon, which took two centuries to build, and for which huge stones had to be brought from Aswan in Egypt; or the Temple of Amon which the ancient Egyptians built at Karnak which covers an area of 5,800 square yards and contains huge columns, each 78 feet high. These temples, built by the followers of pagan religions, were the most enormous ever raised by human beings, with a great deal of effort and expenditure. The reason behind this was that the magicians and clergy wanted to overwhelm the people into their submission and control.

One can then consider and admire the simplicity of the Kaʿba which though situated in the greatest of Islamic mosques, was merely a small room in the midst of a large arid valley. It is also reported that the Prophet described his mosque in Madinah as "pieces of wood and rushes, a bower like that of my brother Moses [Mūsā]," which has been interpreted as meaning that time and money should not be spent on making a building lavish. Indeed, his mosque was built of sun-dried bricks and clay, and the roof, made of palm branches and rushes, came only a few inches above the heads of the tallest of the Companions. Muḥammad al-Ghazālī describes its utter simplicity as follows:

> The mosque was completed within the bounds of simplicity. The floor was sand and pebbles, the roof of palm branches, the pillars of palm trunks. When it rains, the floor becomes muddy. Stray dogs may be seen going in and out...This modest and simple building fostered the human angels, the tamers of giants, and the kings of the hereafter. In this mosque, the Most Gracious permitted the Prophet to guide with the Qur'an the select who believed in his message, educating them with the divine principles from daybreak to nightfall.[18]

It seems that the weaker the relationship between the Muslims and their Creator, the greater their interest in building and decorating mosques at the expense of purifying and refining their souls. In this connection, Muḥammad al-Ghazālī continues:

But when some people failed to build souls on sublime morals, they found the substitute in building lofty mosques to house pigmy worshippers. But the great forefathers left aside the exaggerated decoration of mosques to pay more attention to the reformation and refinement of their souls.[19]

In this chapter, I have presented an outline of the four stages through which believers pass in their journey from perception to cognition: sensory perception, appreciation, then awe-inspiring contemplation and cognition. However, people's contemplation does not have to be limited to the contemplation of beautiful or exquisitely constructed objects in this universe, which contains both the beautiful and the ugly, the great and the insignificant, the good and the evil. Perception can also involve painful, frightening or disturbing experiences, even if appreciation will be emotionally to the contrary. Contemplation can concentrate on the lessons learned from unpleasant experiences, and teach the contemplator how to avoid them, fear them or hate them. In this respect, the Qur'an mentions the story of Qārūn who, like many an evil tyrant, was destroyed by the Almighty so that believers can contemplate his destiny and learn a lesson from it:

Qārūn was doubtless, of the people of Moses; but he acted insolently towards them. Such were the treasures We had bestowed on him, that their very keys would have been a burden to a body of strong men. "Behold, his people said to him, exult not, for God loves not those who exult [in riches]. But seek, with the [wealth] which God had bestowed on you, the home of the hereafter, and do not forget your portion in this world; and do good, as God has been good to you; and do not seek [occasions for] mischief in the land, for God does not love those who do mischief." He said: "This has been given to me because of a certain knowledge which I have." Did he not know that God had destroyed before him [whole] generations which were superior to him in strength and greater in amount [of riches] they had collected? But the wicked are not called [immediately] to account for their sins. So he went forth among his people in the [pride of his worldly] glitter. Those whose aim is the life of this world said: "If only we had the like of what Qārūn has got,

> for he is truly a lord of mighty fortune!" But those who had been granted [true] knowledge said: "Alas for you! The reward of God [in the hereafter] is best for those who believe and work righteousness; but this none shall attain save those who steadfastly persevere [in good]." Then We caused the earth to swallow him up and his house, and he had not [the least little] party to help him against God, nor could he defend himself. And those who had envied his position the day before, began to say on the morrow: "It is indeed God who enlarges or restricts the provision of those of His servants He pleases! Had it not been that God was gracious to us, He could have caused the earth to swallow us up! Those who reject God will assuredly never prosper." (28:76–82)

Similar catastrophes happen all the time without our pondering on God's plan, and merely attributing the events to circumstance or fate. Many dictators have been brought down by those they employed to protect them, and several contemporary scholars later turned to alcohol or drugs, which affected their livers and brains and caused them to hallucinate.[20]

In fact, witnessing terrifying scenes or undergoing personal hardships lead one to contemplate and learn lessons probably in a more effective manner than when one is prompted by a placid appreciation of the beauty, size and precision of a building.

In this connection, I would like to relate a personal experience concerning the lessons that can be learned from a painful or gruesome observation. A young man who used to live in a mosque near our house died on a Thursday, when the mosque was closed for some repair work. His death, therefore, was not discovered until Saturday morning. When I came with a group of people to lift the body and take it to be prepared for burial, we found the spot infested with worms and dampness. The effect of all I had read about death and all my previous contemplation about the insignificance of life was nothing in comparison with the feeling I experienced in those awesome moments.

After the discussion about contemplation from the perspective of thinking and meditation, I shall, in the next chapter, consider the different levels of contemplation achieved through these diverse means.

CHAPTER THREE

Islamic Contemplation and Modern Meditation Procedures

As stated in Chapter One, studying Islamic contemplation from a psychological perspective entails firstly examining meditation procedures and their confirmed ability to help contemplators by positively altering their states of consciousness. However, as previously stressed, in Islamic contemplation these useful altered states are not an end in themselves because the main aim of meditation as an Islamic form of worship is cognitive, intellectual and spiritual: to elevate the Muslims' cognizance of their Creator. These cognitive aspects, which were mentioned in Chapter Two, will now be discussed in detail; Chapter Four will then examine the value of Islamic contemplation as a useful meditative procedure.

The practice of transcendental meditation and similar procedures has become extremely popular in Europe and America in recent years – a phenomenon unprecedented in the history of these nations. This came about after it was established that this kind of meditation, which has ancient oriental and Indian roots, had very positive effects in the treatment of maladies connected with emotional, cognitive and physical disorders. This chapter will discuss the proven benefits of meditation and how they are related to contemplation as an Islamic form of worship.

If one examines the teachings, legislation and prescribed forms of worship of Islam, one notices that all divine enjoinments imply a benefit to the Muslim in the hereafter as well as in this world. Modern advances in medicine and psychophysiological sciences have effectively verified this claim. The value and wisdom of the Islamic prohibitions of alcohol, drugs, fornication and sodomy are too obvious to dwell upon in the modern era of addictions and the AIDS pandemic.[1] In fact, alcohol and drugs are the main dangers facing modern civilization, in both the East and the West: American scientists assert that alcoholism has become their 'number one problem' and is the third cause of death after heart attacks and cancer. They also confess that their nation is spending billions of dollars every year on fighting alcoholism and treating addicts, in addition to the thousands of accidents caused by drunk or drugged drivers, and the fact that the nation is deprived of the contribution of millions of potential workers because they are unable to work. In this respect, I. S. Bengelsdorf, as quoted by R. C. Carson, affirms that the use and abuse of alcohol:

> ...has killed more people, sent more victims to hospitals, generated more police arrests, broken more marriages and homes, and cost industry more money than has the abuse of heroine, amphetamines, barbiturates, and marijuana combined.[2]

Modern medical research has also shown that all the other Islamic prescriptions, rules and desirable behavior have their undisputed value in protecting the physical and psychological health of believers. For example, bodily cleanliness, which believers acquire as a result of ablution (*wuḍū'*) before the five daily prayers, the ceremonial bathing, (*ghusl*) before Friday prayers and after marital intercourse, and other Sunnah practices, have their obvious sanitary aspects. Similar invaluable benefits are seen in every practice performed by Muslims whether in their worship or general exercise of Islamic teachings: for example, the physical exercise in performing the five daily prayers, the health values of fasting and the avoidance of overeating that leads to obesity – which are mentioned in several sayings of the Prophet, and in the following Qur'anic verse: "Eat and drink, but waste not by excess" (7:31).

This inevitably leads us to ask about the value of contemplation and meditation, as forms of worship, to the physical and psychological health of believers. Even without going into the particular case of Islamic contemplation, hundreds of books and research papers published in the late twentieth century stress the value of meditation combined with the faith factor in treating psychological, psychophysiological and organic disorders such as stress, anxiety, insomnia, hypertension, migraine and high cholesterol levels. Modern psychosomatic studies affirm that thinking and other cognitive activities – which are the backbone of contemplation – have a remarkable role in a person's tendency to various maladies, and that suitable contemplation and meditation can bring about a change in their pathological thinking and restore health. Herbert Benson calls this 'cognitive restructuring'.[3] It confirms the old Arabic saying: "Do not pretend sickness, for you may become sick in reality, and die as a result."

The effect of mood and psychological experiences on the organic and physical aspects of a human being is a noticeable everyday occurrence. When people are excited or anxious, their hearts beat faster and they show the other physiological changes and facial expressions associated with excitement or fear. Similarly, when they are overwhelmed with shyness, they blush – that is, if they have the fair complexion that betrays this emotion. Nevertheless, these everyday minor physical changes may not convince many people, including organically minded medical practitioners, about the fundamental role played by thinking and cognitive factors in the formation of human physiology.[4]

A more dramatically convincing proof comes from medical specialists who study the complex physiological phenomena which occur in the body as a result of acute emotional and cognitive stress. One such phenomenon is false pregnancy or pseudocyesis, which occurs when a sterile woman intensely desires to be pregnant and her mind 'orders' her body to react physiologically as though she had conceived: her monthly period stops, her abdomen swells, and her breasts become larger with pigmented tender nipples which begin to secrete milk. According to Benson, some women may even have the sensation of a kicking fetus during the fourth or fifth month of this deceptive phenomenon![5] However, when the women discover that their pregnancy is false, all these physiological changes disappear astonishingly quickly. False pregnancy is one of the oldest known psychosomatic conditions, and was first described by Hippocrates, the ancient father of medicine, yet it is still of relatively frequent occurrence in our modern era. Paul Fried and his colleagues at Jefferson Medical College and Hospital in Philadelphia affirm that the symptoms of women with pseudopregnancy were so impressive that a number of doctors were convinced about their authenticity.[6]

Other significant phenomena are seen in the improvement in the physical health of many patients who are given pills and capsules that, unknown to them, contain no active substance. These capsules may only contain some sugar, but the physician assures the patients that they are of guaranteed benefit. Similarly, the physician may inject a patient with a saline solution, claiming that the injection contains a very potent cure for his physical condition. Research has shown that patients treated in this way, which is known as the 'placebo effect', improve to a degree that is almost equal to those who receive real medication.

A very interesting and revealing study in this connection is reported by S. Wolf, and shows how the patient's belief can even reverse the effect of drugs. His sample was composed of women who suffered from nausea and vomiting during the early months of their pregnancy. He gave them a drug in the form of a syrup which actually caused vomiting but told them that it would cure their condition. Predictably, their nausea and vomiting disappeared and their stomach contractions returned to normal.[7]

Scientists have recently become more interested in this subject, especially after it was proved that a person's cognitive and emotional activities have a direct effect on the immune system. Modern research has conclusively shown that chronic psychological stress, which is collateral with anxiety, depression, severe loneliness, and loss of self-confidence, has a serious effect on human immunity against all diseases. Indeed, chronic stress impels the adrenal glands to increase the output of hormones which, in turn, weaken natural immunity. These hormones, which create a state of emergency of fight or flight in the body, can also elevate blood pressure and strain the heart, and can even cause strokes due to the bursting of blood vessels.

Similar research has led to the emergence of a new discipline, psychoneuro-immunology, which brings together two different fields of specialization for the first time, namely, the field of social sciences and psychology, and that of the chemistry of human immunology.[8] Intensive research has been conducted to improve people's physical health by changing their ideas, feelings and emotions. Some scholars have called this 'the third revolution' in modern Western medicine – the first being the development of surgery and, the second, the discovery of penicillin and other antibiotics. The reason behind this, as previously mentioned, is that what formulates people's thinking and cognitive activity is not the events and stimuli to which they are directly exposed in their environment, but their evaluation and conceptualization of those events and experiences. Epictetus, the Roman philosopher of the first century AC, is reported to have said: "It is not the things around man that are the cause of his disturbance, but his ideas about these things."[9] Thus, it is not only valid to state, as the Arabic saying goes, that "the healthy mind is in the healthy body," but also that "the healthy body is in the healthy mind."

How do meditation and the concurrent relaxation help in the treatment of physical and psychological disorders? The directions which the physician or therapist gives to the patient sound rather too simple and naïve, yet generally their benefit is quickly achieved. These simple meditative instructions were known and followed by Hindus and Buddhists thousands of years ago. Many experimental studies conducted in clinics and medical laboratories, using the latest methods in measuring psychophysiological changes, have proved that concentrative meditation such as transcendental meditation is really a medical revolution in which patients use their mental, cognitive and spiritual powers in curing their ailments and enriching their psychological life.

I shall mention some of these simple instructions from one of the most popular books in this field. Its author, Benson, has become a prominent specialist in meditation and relaxation techniques that have been adapted from yoga and other Eastern practices.[10] Benson asks his patients to sit comfortably and relaxed in a quiet place, to close their eyes, and breathe deeply and quietly, concentrating on the process of breathing. Then they are asked to choose a word or a short sentence from their beliefs or religious faith and to repeat it, contemplating its meaning systematically every time they exhale. If the patients prefer to choose a meaning or a visual form instead of a word or a phrase, then they can do so, following the same repetitive procedure.

When the Americans became interested in transcendental meditation, they adopted it verbatim from the ancient Hindu traditions, and would repeat a meaningless word, or a Hindu or ancient oriental mantra unknown to them. However, it was later realized that the repetition of meaningful expressions which are of religious significance to the meditators, or recall some of their beliefs, have a greater effect by deepening their meditation and intensifying their cure.

Research on transcendental meditation shows that concentration on and constant repetition of words or mental images from their beliefs have a great value for the meditators. It leads them to a deeper understanding and new conceptualization of the subject of their contemplation, and will also raise them to a higher level of abstract and spiritual meanings which they could not have realized otherwise, owing to the monotony of everyday life and the insipid familiarity of their environment. Hence the term 'transcendental meditation'.

An important direction that meditators have to follow is to ignore all the ideas and notions that constantly and compulsively force themselves into their consciousness, disrupting their concentration on the object of meditation. They must resume concentration, and take a passive and relaxed attitude towards these 'intruders' until, in time, they are able to master this exercise. Indeed, with repeated sessions, their contemplation and meditation will deepen, their bodies will be more relaxed and the negative intruding thoughts will greatly decrease. Eventually, they will find that they no longer suffer from the stress, anxiety, and even the physical symptoms about which they used to complain. Several researchers, including Benson, have found that those who perform this contemplation twice a day, for 15 to 20 minutes each session, will notice a marked improvement in their psychological and physical symptoms, and become more optimistic, more productive, and more capable of creative thinking.[11]

This improvement can be proved by certain physiological measurements like the decrease in blood pressure and cholesterol level, and it allows physicians to reduce or even stop the medication taken by their patients – even the chronically ill who used the drugs for years before practising transcendental meditation. In this connection, Benson mentions that the cholesterol level in the blood of patients who practised relaxation and meditation connected with the faith factor was reduced by 35 per cent in comparison with patients who had not undergone treatment by meditation.[12] Similar research shows that the patient's pulse rate is reduced by a significant three beats per minute, and that the consumption of oxygen and blood glucose is equally lessened. On the other hand, the alpha waves on the electroencephalogram, which are affected by tranquillity and relaxation, are found to increase.

Another important measurement of psychophysiological change is the variation in the resistance of the skin to a weak electric current, and is known as the measurement of the psychogalvanic skin response. Such resistance to an electric current, which is too small to be felt by the person under test, decreases with the increase of perspiration and humidity in the palm of the human hand, and vice versa. Thus, when a person is anxious, and the sweat glands in the palm secrete more sweat, the moist hand becomes a better conductor for the mild electric current; whereas when the person is relaxed, the dry palm offers a greater resistance to the current. The results can be recorded easily by attaching special electrodes to a person's palm and feeding the resulting electric current to a specialized instrument or computer. In his book, *How to Meditate,* L. Le Shan says that transcendental meditation brings about a condition directly opposed to that of anxiety and anger, and that it increases the resistance of the skin by more than 400 per cent.[13]

The convincing evidence from these psychophysical measurements is further supported by the dramatic reports given by the meditators themselves: headaches, chronic digestive disorders, chest pains and other psychophysiological symptoms are reported to disappear; insomnia, stress and anxiety simply evaporate. Even if the physical symptoms do not disappear completely, they weaken considerably so that the patient becomes generally less concerned about them.

Among the important psychological changes affirmed by meditators, whether sick or healthy, is the immense feeling of tranquillity that envelops them. They also report a strong sense of self-knowledge and a close affinity with the created order, a warm feeling towards others, a great optimism, and a growing ability for productive effort and creative thinking. Many meditators also compare this feeling to that of someone coming home after many years abroad.

Le Shan affirms that these ambiguous feelings that are situated beyond the physical world are not fanciful or self-inspired – a fact strongly confirmed by the similarity of the reports of ascetics, worshippers and mystics from all parts of the world throughout history. To secure further evidence for his claim, Le Shan appeals to physics. He writes:

> If we have learned one thing from modern physics, it is that there may be two viewpoints about something which are mutually contradictory and yet both viewpoints are equally 'correct'. In physics this is called the principle of complementarity. It states that for the fullest understanding of some phenomena we must approach them from two different viewpoints. Each viewpoint by itself tells only half the truth.[14]

In support of this quotation, we must remember that Einstein's relativity theory and quantum physics shattered the clockwork image of the universe as propounded by Newton. In fact, new physics clearly demonstrated that what appears to be one thing may turn out to be its opposite. At the subatomic level, what may be experimentally demonstrated to be particles or entities that are restricted to a very tiny volume are also shown to behave like waves that stretch out over a wide area of space, and there is ample evidence for both contradictory concepts – a fact which confused many physicists when it was first discovered. Einstein's relativity theory also overturned our concept of mass and time. The former is now viewed as concentrated energy that can detonate as the mushroom of an atomic explosion, and the latter has simply become a fourth dimension. If all this can happen on the material level of knowledge, then one should not be surprised that, as Le Shan affirms, there exists a higher knowledge of the universe and life which human beings can achieve through meditation.

Thus far I have discussed the negative and positive influences of passions, emotions, beliefs and other cognitive activities that involve the process of contemplation on human psychophysical health. I have summarized several studies that show how people can afflict themselves with psychophysiological maladies or weaken their immunity system to microbial diseases, or how they can cure themselves and raise themselves to a higher level of existence. I have also emphasized the role of contemplation in the West and mentioned some of the simple steps that can be adapted for the practice of meditation as a therapy.

It is not difficult for a Muslim to see the resemblance of this kind of therapeutic meditation with the contemplation of the heavens and the earth and the praise and remembrance of God. Indeed, both practices share a concentration on the object of meditation, and an attempt to eliminate or lessen external and internal interference – that is, whatever may distract the mind – whether external noises or internal intruding notions. They also share a revision and a repetition of meditative meanings with a regular tempo, until the meditator or praising contemplator discovers a new meaning, achieves a novel realization, or experiences an unprecedented vision. They both use deep contemplation to liberate the static sensory perception from the prison of the daily routine of material life and the confines of familiarity, to move freely towards further horizons and a wider scope of knowledge.

The directions given by therapists in the books and educational tapes on meditation and relaxation combined with the use of the faith factor, which have become popular in Europe and America, are similar to those used by a Muslim worshipper, sitting down after performing the ritual prayer (salah), absorbed in contemplating the grace of God, His grandeur and the precision of His creation, incessantly repeating words of praise and glorification of the Almighty. While referring to this obvious similarity, it is interesting to note that Benson not only advises people of all religious faiths to use his meditative techniques, but also suggests the very words or phrases they could repeat when fully relaxed in their meditation. For instance, he writes:

> Moslems might want to repeat words like the following:
>
> - The word for God, *Allah*
> - Some of the words said to be uttered to Mohammed by Allah at the Prophet's initial call: "Thy Lord is wondrous kind..."
> - The words of the first Moslem who called the 'faithful' to prayer. Though his master tortured him by depriving him of water in the desert, he kept repeating *ahadum*, or 'One [God]' until his master relented.[15]

In his last suggestion, Benson was referring to Bilāl, the beloved Companion of the Prophet, although he misread the Arabic word *aḥadun* as *aḥadum*. Of course, Muslims who follow the teachings of the Prophet, by regularly relaxing and contemplating after their five daily prayers, know what focus words to use as they were specified by the Prophet himself. These words and short phrases include "Glory be to God" (*subḥān Allāh*), "Praise be to God" (*alḥamdu li Allāh*) and "God is greater" (*Allāhu akbar*).

It is of interest to note that Benson strongly maintained that after patients become proficient in meditation with the faith factor, they no longer need to lie down or sit in a relaxed position; they can relax and meditate, repeating their focus words of faith, even when walking, jogging or swimming. This reminds one of Islamic contemplation, as in the Qur'an the Almighty praises the believers who remember Him while they are standing, sitting, or lying down on their sides (3:191).

When one considers the obvious similarity between meditation rooted in ancient oriental religions and that of Islamic contemplation, one could accept the theory advanced by Abūl Aᶜlā Mawdūdī that Buddhism and Hinduism may have been revealed faiths, but that, like many other ancient religions, they gradually lost their purity and allegiance to the One God. Thus as the centuries unfolded, nothing remained in these religions but deviant beliefs and rituals of worship.[16] For instance, they retained some rites such as meditation, although it has abandoned its true and original aim of worshipping God and contemplating His creation. The secular and pragmatic Western world then copied these incomplete practices when their medical and psychotherapeutic benefits had been verified, without adopting the true religious objective behind them or even their deviant oriental roots.

As has been previously mentioned, all Islamic rites and forms of worship, and all enjoinments and prohibitions made by the Shariᶜah, have benefits for humankind in this world and in the hereafter. These benefits are known to some and unknown to others. For instance, it is clear that concentration and serious meditation on a spiritual or moral subject would be beneficial to any person. Such benefit would be further multiplied if the contemplation was coupled with the repetition of words and meanings related to the meditator's beliefs. Meditation is also helped if the meditators sink into a state of tranquil relaxation, whereby they cast aside daily occupations and notions, trying to tune in with what is beyond matter, and penetrate beyond the world of the senses. They would also benefit from concentrating their finer senses on the natural sounds and movements in their environment: the twittering of birds, the rustling of trees in the breeze, or even internal regular physical movements like their own breathing or heartbeats – a process called 'mindfulness meditation'. This ability to benefit from meditation is an attribute that God has rooted in human nature so as to enable the individual to worship, glorify and know Him. If people use this gift in the proper spiritual manner, they will achieve its psycho-physiological merits as well as the expected divine reward. If not, they will nevertheless gain its basic benefits.

These benefits, enjoyed by non-Muslims who practice meditation, are similar to those which they would enjoy if they observed various forms of cleanliness, such as brushing their teeth several times a day, washing regularly (as in *wuḍū'* and *ghusl*), and trimming their fingernails; or if they perform light physical exercise as in the Islamic daily prayers, or if they avoid alcohol, drugs, fornication, sodomy and overeating. Practising Muslims do all these useful activities as religious obligatory duties or as followers of the Sunnah of their Prophet. They enjoy their benefit in this world and God's pleasure in the hereafter, whereas non-Muslims simply enjoy the merits of these hygienic and beneficial practices in this world. Sometimes these beneficial practices attract people who, irrespective of race and environment, have a natural, inborn tendency toward such a lifestyle, in the same way as they are drawn to flowing streams, greenery, and physical beauty. Contemplative believers therefore enjoy all these health benefits – physical and psychological – as well as experiencing a much deeper and more advanced contemplation because of their sound faith, profound insight and clarity of religious vision.

Furthermore, practising Muslims often find contemplation a relatively effortless undertaking as they have been accustomed to doing it in their five daily prayers since early childhood. Though the language of the Qur'an is an inimitable Arabic symphony, its short chapters can be understood by children, and they can ponder over the verses that glorify and praise God when they recite them in their prayers. They 'contemplate' within the bounds of their limited experience and incomplete maturity. It is illuminating in this connection to mention that Benson found that these early meditative and spiritual experiences and rituals have very useful health benefits to them as they grow up, even if they stop practising them as adults. He writes:

> Remembered wellness makes the religious ritual a very powerful mechanism. There is something very influential about invoking a ritual that you may first have practiced in childhood, about regenerating the neural pathways that were formed in your youthful experience of faith. In my medical practice, that has proven true, even, I might add, among many adults who have rejected the religion they practiced in their youth.[17]

Benson then goes on to explain the psychoneural mechanisms behind this interesting phenomenon:

> Even if you experience the ritual from an entirely different perspective of maturity and life history, the words you read, the songs you sing, and the prayers you invoke will soothe you in the same way they did in what was perhaps a simpler time in your life. Even if you don't consciously appreciate that there is any real drama or emotion attached to the ritual, the brain retains a memory of the constellation of activities associated with the ritual, both the emotional content that allows the brain to weigh its importance and the nerve cell firings, interactions, and chemical releases that were first activated.[18]

Accordingly, a contemplating, practising Muslim can achieve a high level of meditation with minimum time and energy. Just listening to the poetic words of the Qur'an chanted by a beautiful voice can bring about all the fine meditative responses in a few minutes. After a series of sophisticated experiments conducted at Akbar Clinics in Florida in the United States, Dr. Ahmed Elkadi concluded that when Muslims listen to the recitation of Qur'anic verses, whether they are Arabic speakers or not, they experience all the physiological changes indicative of the release from stress and anxiety, as well as warm feelings of tranquillity and an increase of immunity against disease, and the other changes described earlier about transcendental meditation. In these experiments, Elkadi used the most advanced electronic equipment to measure blood pressure, heartbeat, muscle tension and skin resistance to electric current, and found that the recitation of the Qur'an clearly had a calming effect in 97 per cent of cases. The subjects naturally also experienced a heightened spiritual reaction which he could not measure since there is no 'spiritometer' for measuring this sacred dimension.[19]

These results were supported by doctoral experimental research carried out under my supervision in the University of Khartoum by Dr. Muhammad Khair al-Irgisoosi. He selected a variable that lends itself to accurate physical measurement, namely, the increase or decrease in blood pressure, which was measured by millimeters of mercury. Physicians from the Faculty of Medicine of the University of Khartoum helped by supplying us with patients suffering from essential hypertension, which is high blood pressure caused by a stressful lifestyle or other unknown reasons. The study compared treatment by muscular relaxation combined with verbal supportive therapy to treatment with muscular relaxation combined with Islamic spiritual therapy containing selected verses from the Qur'an and sayings of the Prophet that deal with curing disease. Patients were divided into three groups: an experimental group, a carefully matched control group, and a group that received muscular relaxation training without supportive therapy or readings from the Qur'an.

The results were unequivocal. Though all the patients improved, the rate of improvement in subjects who received relaxation therapy combined with Islamic spiritual therapy was significantly better than the other two groups. This statistically significant improvement was sustained for months after therapy and, in the case of some patients, their doctors told them to stop taking their medication because their blood pressure had returned to its normal level.[20]

Thus it can be stated that the real value of Islamic meditation lies in its connection with the worship, remembrance and glorification of God and pleading for His help. Hence, the similarity between contemplation, as an Islamic form of worship, and other forms of Eastern and Western meditation is in fact only superficial, because the bedrock of Islamic contemplation is the belief in the Oneness of God. It is a rational deep faith that proclaims that the Almighty is the only One Who sustains this universe, from its infinitesimal electron to its most colossal galaxy. This belief is not only the cornerstone of all forms of Islamic meditation, but it is also the very foundation of Islam.

Islamic contemplation is based on the progression from meditating on the creation to its Creator. It is a smooth rational movement, since the Islamic faith is uncorrupted by any association of creatures or objects with the Almighty or any polytheistic deviations.

Atheists may contemplate the immense beauty of the universe with the vague understanding that it is 'Mother Nature' or the 'big bang' that brought it into existence, or they may avoid the issue of how this world came to be what it is altogether. They contemplate with emotional passions, completely disregarding the rational issue of how the universe was created. Likewise, pagans or polytheists who believe that it is many gods, fighting among themselves, who created everything, will find it very difficult to meditate with their rational minds and hearts since these may contradict each other. For this reason, Westerners who wish to have a 'mystical' experience are advised to avoid 'reason-based forms of worship'.[21] Indeed, as Benson says in his comments on Karen Armstrong's book, *A History of God*, this is because the mystical experience is not rational, but "intuitive and non-verbal." Armstrong calls it "silent contemplation". She writes:

> The mystical experience...is a subjective experience that involves an interior journey, not a perception of an objective fact outside the self; it is undertaken through the image making part of the mind – often called imagination – rather than through the more cerebral, logical faculty. Finally, it is something that the mystic creates in himself or herself deliberately.[22]

Le Shan gives the same advice to meditators as Benson and Armstrong. He also cautions the student of meditation: "Try not to be verbal or intellectual about the process. It is a sensing, a putting out 'radar', rather than a process of the intellect."[23]

As for practising Muslims, their contemplation is a spiritual practice in which all their cognitive and spiritual faculties are activated in pursuit of the true cognizance of the Almighty. It is not an irrational or emotional endeavor to cure a disorder, nor a painful exercise in which the body is tortured by standing for several days on one leg or sleeping on beds of sharp nails. Islamic contemplation is a form of worship that binds the heart with the mind, the rational with the emotional, and the sensible with the passionate, so that sober contemplators may be in a better spiritual state in which their prayers, God willing, will be more acceptable. Irrational and highly emotional responses are frowned upon in Islamic contemplation, and altered states of consciousness are not, as previously mentioned, an end in themselves. Likewise, the occasional paranormal experiences that may occur as a result of very deep meditation, and which are so valued by Eastern and Western mystics to the extent that they are prepared to discard reasoning or tolerate severe bodily pain to secure them, are neither sought nor are they objects of excitement in true Islamic contemplation. Furthermore, since many worshippers of Satan can produce paranormal performances, genuine Muslim worshippers and meditators view such phenomena with suspicion. That is why al-Ḥasan al-Baṣrī, in the statement already quoted, considers the conscious remembrance and contemplation of God as two sides of the same coin. Thus one could describe Islamic contemplation, in comparison with atheistic or polytheistic meditation, as two apparently identical seashells – but whereas one contains a rare pearl, the other contains nothing but the remains of an ordinary shellfish.

This, of course, does not mean that the sense of happiness, the psychological calm, the clarity of mind, and the intimacy felt by non-Muslim meditators toward all the beings in this universe are not genuine feelings. Indeed, as stated earlier, it is a therapeutic exercise that can relieve sufferers from their physical and psychological disorders. However, this glimmer of light and peace which non-Muslim meditators experience is a reward for their striving to detach themselves from the materialistic threads of their daily problems. They have a glimpse of the transcendent spiritual horizon, perhaps for the first time in their lives, and realize that it is a great improvement in comparison to their materialistic struggle with life.

This feeling, which has such a great impact on non-Muslim meditators, is, however, hardly comparable to what believers feel, because they know that every atom in this universe glorifies and praises the Almighty. The Qur'an states: "There is not a thing but celebrates His praise; but you [humans] do not understand how they declare His glory" (17:44). Though contemplating believers cannot decipher the glorification of God by the universe, they feel the harmony between their glorification and that of all other creatures. This feeling becomes deeper with the continuation of contemplation until it reaches spiritual sublimity and a sense of joy and spiritual pleasure that is incomparable to any worldly bliss.

Describing this state of bliss, in which the cares and ailments of this world are eliminated, as darkness is eliminated by light, Ibn al-Qayyim says in *Madārij al-Sālikīn*:

> The contemplative believer who remembers God will begin to enjoy solitude and places of seclusion where voices and movements are hushed...There he will find strength of heart and will, and he will no longer be worried or depressed...Then he will begin to taste the sweetness of worship, of which he cannot have enough. In it, he will find abundance of pleasure and comfort – more than what he used to find in diversion and play, or in the satisfaction of worldly desires...When he experiences this state, many of the worldly concerns will disappear, as he is in a completely different world from the rest of humanity.[24]

Similarly, Ibn Taymiyyah quotes in his *Majmūʿ al-Fatāwā* (The Complete Collection of Fatwas) some of the sincere contemplators given to remembrance of God. One of them said: "I used to be in a state where I would say, 'If people in paradise are in a state like this one, then they are indeed in real bliss.'" Another one said: "At times, the heart experiences moments when it dances with glee." A third one said: "The truly vigilant worshippers find much more pleasure in their worship than those given to diversion in their play."[25]

What a difference there is between the practising Muslim contemplators and those atheists and pagans who suffer under numerous layers of darkness, who can reach but a glimpse of these wonders through meditation in their quest of what is beyond perception! It is as though the Qur'an was referring to them when it says: "Whenever the lightning gives them light, they walk therein, and whenever darkness falls around them, they stand still" (2:20).

CHAPTER FOUR

The Qur'an and the Contemplation of God's Creation

The contemplation of God's creation is one of the greatest forms of worship in Islam. It is not surprising, therefore, that many Qur'anic verses encourage this activity and do so using various methods in order to appeal to every temperament and spiritual state. The aim is to divert people away from their dulled senses, bad habits and monotonous familiarity, and encourage them to witness the signs of their Lord in the universe with insight and impressionable hearts. The following are some of the main methods.

INSPIRATION OF THE NATURE OF GOD AND HIS EXALTED ATTRIBUTES

True Islamic contemplation can only spring from a heart that believes in God and a mind that submits to Him and His Exalted Attributes. This is the unwavering faith of oneness (*tawḥīd*), which is to bear witness that the Almighty is the One and only God Who created, governs and sustains the universe. Any other form of contemplation of the beauty and splendor of the heavens and the earth would be considered as atheism or polytheism (*shirk*) because the contemplator would not be recognizing, let alone praising and thanking the Creator. For this reason, the Qur'an often repeats this doctrine through the mention of God's Exalted Attributes:

> Say: "He is God, the One; God, the Eternal, Absolute. He does not beget nor is He begotten, and there is none like Him." (112:1–5)

> God is He; Whom there is no god but Him. He knows all things, both secret and open. He is the Most Gracious, the Most Merciful. God is

> He; there is no god but Him. The Sovereign, the Holy One, the Source of Peace and Perfection, the Guardian of Faith and Preserver of Safety; the Exalted in Might, the Irresistible, the Supreme. Glory be to God! So High is He above the partners they [the infidels] attribute to Him. He is God, the Creator, the Evolver and the Bestower of forms. To Him belong the most Beautiful Names. Whatever is in the heavens and the earth declares His praises and glory. He is the Exalted in Might, the Wise. (59:22–24)

> God is the Originator of the heavens and the earth. How can He have a son when He has no companion? He created all things and has full knowledge of all things. That is God, your Lord! There is no god but Him, the Creator of all things. So worship Him. He has power to dispose of all affairs. No vision can grasp Him, but His Grasp is over all visions. He is above all comprehension, yet is acquainted with all things. (6:101–103)

It is essential to establish this strong uncorrupted faith in God before embarking on the spiritual journey of Islamic contemplation, for it will be a guiding light to the believer as well as a firm root preventing him from being led astray. The Qur'an also uses other arguments to guide the believers on their spiritual expedition. These are often powerful images that act like reminders for those who are still reluctant and have hardened hearts.

REMINDERS OF THE FAVORS OF GOD

The Qur'an attempts to soften human hearts in many ways. One of these is by mentioning the grace and favors of God. Contemplation of these can generate a feeling of compassionate mercy and love.

> And He has created cattle for you. From them you derive warmth and numerous benefits, and of their [meat] you eat. (16:5)

> It is He Who sends down rain from the sky. From it you drink, and out of it grows the vegetation on which you feed your cattle. And with it He

produces for you corn, olives, date palms, grapes and every kind of fruit. Verily in this is a sign for those who give thought. (16:10–11)

He has made subject to you the night and the day, the sun and the moon, and the stars are in subjection by His command. Verily in this are signs for men who are wise. And the things on this earth which He has multiplied in varying colors [and qualities]. Verily in this is a sign for men who celebrate the praises of God [in gratitude]. It is He Who has made the sea subject, so that you may eat thereof flesh that is fresh and tender, and that you may extract from it ornaments to wear. And you see the ships on it that plough the waves, so that you may seek of the bounty of God, and that you may be grateful. And He has set up on the earth mountains, standing firm, lest it should shake with you, and rivers and roads, so that you may guide yourselves; and marks and signposts. And by the stars [men] guide themselves. Is then He Who creates like one that creates not? Will you not receive admonition? If you would count the favors of God, never would you be able to number them, for God is Oft-Forgiving, Most Merciful. (16:12–18)

This reminder to contemplate the mercy and love of God towards humankind and all other creatures that inhabit this globe immediately moves the hearts of those who are sensitive, appreciative and wise. As for those whose eyes and hearts are closed to the divine call for contemplation, the Qur'an describes them in verses such as the following:

Say: "Look at [and contemplate] what is in the heavens and the earth." But neither signs nor warners profit those who do not believe. (10:101)

And how many signs in the heavens and the earth do they pass by? Yet they turn their faces away from them. (12:105)

The countless signs of God's marvelous creation, as Yūsuf ʿAlī records in his comment on the last verse, "are scattered literally throughout nature – throughout creation – for all who have eyes to see.

And yet man is so arrogant that he turns his very eyes away from them."[1] Such insensitive, unrelenting hearts require a harsher approach to shake their unreasonable attitude.

REPRIMANDS FOR UNRELENTING HEARTS

The tone of these addresses are often violent and coupled with threats. Most of these verses begin with the question "Have they not seen?" or "Do they not see?"

> Have they not seen what is before them and behind them, of the sky and the earth? If We wished, We could cause the earth to swallow them up, or cause a piece of the sky to fall upon them. In this there is a sign for every devotee that turns to God [in repentance]. (34:9)

> Do they not look at the camels, how they were made? And at the sky, how it was raised? And at the mountains, how they were fixed? And at the earth, how it was spread out? (88:17–20)

Many such verses come from the Qur'anic narratives or from the words of the prophets. For example, Noah (Nūḥ) reprimanded the unbelievers among his people with the following words:

> What is the matter with you, that you do not believe in God or fear God's Majesty, seeing that it is He Who created you in diverse stages? Do you not see how God has created the seven heavens one above another and made the moon a light in their midst, and made the sun a [glorious] lamp? (71:13–16)

PRAISE FOR THE PIOUS

Conversely, some verses offer encouragement and praise to the mentally alert, who see nothing in the world that does not teach them a lesson and remind them of the innumerable favors of God. These are the pious who remember God in every psychological or physical state of their psyche and body:

> Behold! In the creation of the heavens and the earth, and the alternation of night and day, there are indeed signs for men of understanding – men who celebrate the praise of God, standing, sitting, and lying down on their sides, and contemplate the wonders of the creation in the heavens and the earth. O Lord, You have not created this for naught! Glory be to You! Give us salvation from the torment of fire [in the hereafter]. (3:190–191)

APPEALS TO THE INNATE AESTHETIC SENSE

The Qur'an also urges people to contemplate the Divine signs in the universe by awakening the innate aesthetic sense in them. The following verses, aim to arouse people's genuine feelings and emotions so as to enable them to observe the beauty of everything on the earth – whether the various colors and shades, plants, animals, or even inanimate objects:

> Do you not see that God has sent down rain from the sky, whereby We have brought out produce of various colors. And in the mountains are tracts white and red, of various shades of colors, and black intense in hue. And similarly among men and crawling creatures and cattle who all have various colors. Those who truly fear God among His servants are those who have knowledge. For God is Exalted in Might, and is Oft-Forgiving. (35:27–28)

We also find verses where the Almighty, after showing His favors to humanity in creating the cattle for their sustenance and use, reminds His slaves to contemplate their beauty:

> And He has created cattle for you. From them you derive warmth and numerous benefits, and of their [meat] you eat. And you have a sense of beauty in them as you drive them home in the evening and as you lead them forth to pasture in the morning. (16:5–6)

> He Who has made everything which He has created most good and beautiful, He began the creation of man with clay. (32:7)

In his important work, *Fī Ẓilāl al-Qur'ān* (In the Shade of the Qur'an), Sayyid Quṭb interprets this last verse in the following moving words:

> This world is beautiful, inexhaustibly beautiful. Man may grasp and enjoy this beauty as much as he wishes, and as much as the Creator of this world wishes. The element of beauty in this world is intentional. Perfection of creation results in achieving beauty. The perfection of creation is apparent in the beauty of every organ and every creature. Look at the bee, the flower, the star, the night, the morning, the shades, the clouds, this music pervading the entire universe, this perfect and whole harmony. It is a pleasant journey in this universe of beauty and perfection. The Qur'an draws our attention to all this, so we may ponder and enjoy it. Hence: "He Who has made everything which He has created most good," is a verse which arouses the heart to trace the aspects of beauty and perfection in this great universe.[2]

THE ALMIGHTY'S OWN FAITH IN HIS CREATION

However, the most important point which elevates the status of contemplation is that God Himself swears by some of His creation. This is the greatest call to ponder over this creation, probe its depths, and think deeply about its content. The Almighty swears by the dawn, the mid-morning, the twilight, the moon, the figs and the olives; he swears by the winds, the stars, the sky, the break of day and the descending night.

There is no doubt that the high status accorded by Islam to contemplation is what led worshippers and ascetics such as al-Ḥasan al-Baṣrī to assert that "one hour of contemplation is better than a whole night's vigil in worship" and for the Umayyad caliph ʿUmar ibn ʿAbd al-ʿAzīz to say that "remembrance of God is a good deed, but contemplation of God's favors is the best form of worship."[3]

ISLAMIC ENCOURAGEMENT TO SELF-CONTEMPLATION

People's ignorance of themselves and their failure to contemplate and study the affairs of humankind are considered by Islam to be glaring examples of negligence and a lack of observance of one of God's greatest signs in the universe. When Islam urges people to contemplate the heavens, the seas, the mountains and the rivers, and to meditate on what God created for the benefit of humanity, what, then, can be said about meditation on the creation of the human being, before whom God made His angels prostrate, and to whom He subjected whatever existed in the heavens and on the earth?

> And He has subjected to you, as [a gift] from Himself, all that is in the heavens and on the earth. Behold, in that are signs indeed for those who reflect. (45:13)

While there are many Qur'anic verses which encourage meditation on the heavens and the earth in general, and where the human being is considered the most important creation, there are also many verses which are specifically concerned with contemplating the creation of humankind. As previously mentioned, the Qur'an uses every means to arouse human hearts from their dulled senses and monotonous familiarity, in order to witness the signs of the Lord in the heavens and on the earth with alertness and enlightened insight. The verses concerning humankind follow similar methods of encouragement in order to suit every heart and every emotional state.

The following verses are examples detailing the creation of man, and the favors that God bestowed on those with soft hearts:

> We created man from a quintessence of clay; then we placed him as [a drop of] sperm in a place of rest, firmly fixed. Then We made the [drop of] sperm into a clot of congealed blood. Then of the clot We made a [fetus] lump; then We made from that lump bones, and clothed the bones with flesh; then We developed from it another creature. So blessed be God, the best Creator. (23:12–14)

> Say: "It is He Who has created you [and made you grow], and made for you the faculties of hearing, seeing, feeling and understanding. But little thanks do you show." (67:23)

As for the cruel-hearted and the arrogant, the Qur'an addresses them with similar reproachful questions:

> Does not man see that it is We Who created him from sperm? Yet, behold [how he stands forth] as an open adversary! (36:77)

> Have We not created you from a fluid [held] despicable which We placed in an abode of rest, firmly fixed, for a determined period [of gestation]? For We do determine and We are the best to determine. Woe on that Day to those who reject the truth! (77:20–24)

Concerning the arousing of the aesthetic aspect of human nature, the Almighty says:

> We have indeed created man in the best of moulds. (95:4)

> He has created the heavens and the earth in just proportions, and has given you shape, and made your shapes beautiful, and to Him is the final goal. (64:3)

Just as God swears by some of His cosmic signs and creations on earth, He also swears by the human soul; sometimes it is in the context of His cosmic signs, and at other times in connection with the Day of Judgment, thus exalting the human soul to the highest level. *Sūrah al-Qiyāmah* opens with this glorious oath:

> I swear by the Day of Resurrection, and I swear by the reproachful soul. Does man think that we cannot assemble his bones? Nay, we are able to put together in perfect order the very shape of his fingers. (75:1–4)

The divine oath may also come as a vow to create the well-proportioned human self and to inspire it with life after referring to the universe, where God swears by the sun, the moon, the day, the night, the firmament, and the levelled earth:

> By the soul, and the order given to it, and the enlightenment as to its

wrong and its right – truly he who purifies it will prosper, and he who corrupts it will fail. (91:7–10)

The Almighty also makes an oath by other aspects that relate to humankind. For instance, in a short but comprehensive surah, God swears by the short lifespan of humankind on the face of the earth, after which a human being will be either raised to high levels of bliss or sunk into perdition:

By the mid-afternoon [or the short lifetime], man is really in loss – except those who have faith and do righteous deeds, and join in the mutual teaching of truth, and of patience and constancy. (103:1–3)

God also swears by His Exalted Being to assert the truthfulness of the Qur'an, and exemplifies it by one of the most important gifts He has bestowed upon human beings, namely, their ability to speak and communicate with one another:

Then, by the Lord of the heaven and the earth, this [Qur'an] is the very truth, as true as the fact that you can speak. (51:23)

These, then, are some of the Qur'anic verses which encourage people to contemplate upon themselves. In fact, if there were nothing to denote the wonder of God's creation in the universe except human beings, that would be sufficient to force them into absolute submission to their Creator. Indeed, people will always be mystified by their soul, their spirit and their mind, which are the very creations that distinguish them as human beings. Although these are only some of their components, they cannot be embodied in time or place, and will thus remain beyond human comprehension. To realize that they are unable to understand fully their identity is, alone, the greatest challenge that calls people to submission and modesty.

Even the simpler psychological phenomena whose effects can be recorded in the laboratory – like learning, memory, emotions and motivations – are still not fully grasped by psychology. The latter only touches on the external aspects of their infinite depths, like a child playing near the shores of an endless ocean. Furthermore, the tangible biological and material aspects of humankind can only be understood at the superficial level. Even if the entire human race were to spend all its life investigating the signs of God in the human body, it could only scratch the surface. As previously mentioned, the human brain is still the most enigmatic thing in this universe. All the bewildering achievements of science have only increased people's astonishment at the complexity of the biological computer carried inside the human skull. Benson writes in *Timeless Healing*:

> [the brain] is so complex, so constantly in motion, so megafaceted and super-connected that all our attempts to describe its actions are, by nature, simplistic. Every remarkable discovery we make only further elucidates how astonishingly elaborate is the brain and its circuitry – that which affords us life and health, movement and memory, intuition and wisdom. That which appears to be a crude clump of jelly assembles and then retains notes on every movement, every breath, every incident that has ever occurred to you or ever will, as well as every thought or dream you have ever had or ever will have.[4]

Therefore, the divine call, which questions how people can be blind to the miraculous creation of their own selves – "And in your own selves, do you not see?" (51:21) – will always remain as new and challenging as when it was first revealed. To expound further on the meaning of this verse, it may be useful to conclude this chapter with a quotation from Sayyid Quṭb:

> "And in your own selves, do you not see?" Man is the greatest wonder on this earth, but he is inattentive to his own worth and inherent mysteries when his heart is inattentive to faith, and when he is denied the favors of certitude. He is a wonder in his body formation: in the secrets of this body, in his spiritual formation and in the mysteries of his soul. He is a wonder within and without, as he represents the elements of this universe.
>
> You claim you are a microcosm
> While you contain the macrocosm.

Whenever man contemplates himself, he is faced with astonishing and bewildering mysteries: the formation of his organs, their positions and functions; the way the functions are executed; the mysteries of his soul, and its known and unknown energies; how he forms his concepts and the way they are stored and remembered. All these images...where and how are they stored? These images, visions and sights...how are they recalled? What is unknown of these images is immeasurably more. Then there are the mysteries of humankind, in its propagation and succession: one cell carries all the characteristics of the humankind, including those of the parents and forefathers. Yet where do all these characteristics lie, in such a tiny cell? And how does that cell recreate them minutely, ending with a reproduction of this wonderful human being?[5]

CHAPTER FIVE

Contemplation as an Unrestricted Form of Worship

Contemplation of the creation of the heavens and the earth and all that is included in them is a practice which cannot be impeded by changes in time, place or the nature of things. It is a free, unrestrained form of worship. It is also a cognitive and emotional process that enlivens the heart and enlightens perception as the mind ascends from contemplating the signs of God in the universe to their Creator and Lord. This is the real meaning of contemplation.

Concerning the liberation of contemplation from the limits of time and place, the Qur'an encourages the practice of contemplation of the beginning of creation: "Say: 'Travel through the earth and see how God originated creation. Thus will God produce a later creation, for God has power over all things'" (29:20). In addition to encouraging believers to contemplate the present, the Qur'an invites them to contemplate the destinies of extinct nations: "Do they not travel on the earth, and see what was the end of those before them? They were superior to them in strength..." (30:9). While ordering the believers to contemplate this world, the Qur'an also calls for meditation on the hereafter: "...Thus God makes clear to you His signs, in order that you may consider [their bearing] on this life and the hereafter" (2:219–220). This is because contemplation limited to the transient world is nothing but an incomplete image of the universe and a distorted concept of the reality of human existence. Therefore, the believer is ordered to contemplate God's creation from the beginning until the Day of Judgment.

Concerning the freedom of contemplation, the Qur'an calls for meditation on the natural creations of God in which the human hand plays no part, such as the heavens, the mountains and the seas. The Qur'an also draws the believers' attention to the bounties with which people have been favored, such as the inventions which God has enabled some to achieve in order to serve humanity:

> Behold! In the creation of the heavens and the earth; in the alternation of the night and the day; in the sailing of the ships across the ocean for the profit of mankind; in the rain which God sends down from the skies, and the life which he gives therewith to an earth that is dead; in the beasts of all kinds that He scatters through the earth; in the change of the winds, and the clouds that are trailed between the sky and the earth – there are indeed signs for the wise. (2:164)

Although some of these achievements and inventions – like the sailing ships – are the work of human beings, it is the Almighty Who favored them with the knowledge that made such achievements possible:

> ...Nor shall they attain any of His knowledge except that which He wills... (2:255)

> It was We Who taught him [Prophet David] the making of coats of mail [defensive armor] for your benefit, to guard you from each other's violence. So will you then be grateful? (21:80)[1]

Moreover, no human discovery or invention can ever occur outside the natural laws established by God. In fact, human feats are nothing but a clarification of the significance of these laws. The Almighty has ascribed to His Exalted Being the ownership of the huge ships that sail across the oceans like moving mountains: "And to Him belong the ships, sailing smoothly across the seas, lofty as mountains" (55:24). Not only do the ships belong to Him, but also the aircrafts, rockets, satellites, and all the other things that men and women have made and discovered by God's will and grace: "Your Lord is He that makes the ship go smoothly for you across the sea, so that you may seek of His bounty. He is to you Most Merciful" (17:66).

It is unfortunate nowadays that some believers do not contemplate modern inventions simply because they are the products of countries that do not believe in Islam or in the Oneness of God. At the same time, they see how the Muslim world has become a weak consumer of modern inventions and services, and how it has been violated and overrun by the modern military technology of aggressive non-Muslim countries. In the midst of such emotional confusion, some believers entertain divided feelings, as on one hand they can see the power, mercy, and great bounties of God in His natural creations like rivers and mountains and, on the other hand, they see the great inventions of modern technology – some of which stimulate in them quite negative responses. Various propagators of Western and Eastern trends of thought have encouraged this tendency to an extent that the distinction between the natural creations of God and the modern inventions of humankind has almost become a split between science and religion.

However, when their hearts move closer to God and they have a clearer vision of the universe, people realize that the globe and all it contains represent but an insignificant atom in the infinite domain of God. Moreover, God says in the Qur'an that it is He Who created human beings and whatever the human mind and hands have made: "God has created you and your handiwork" (37:96). In fact, one of the reasons for the degrading situation of the Muslim world today is its disregard of the laws of God on earth.

It should be remembered, in this connection, that when God drew the attention of the people of Makkah, Madinah and the neighboring areas to the ships sailing smoothly across the oceans like moving mountains, it was at a time when most of these ships were in the hands of people who had not yet embraced Islam. Nevertheless, it did not prevent the believers from contemplating a sign of God, the benefit and use of which He had chosen to put into the hands of unbelievers.

This short chapter has shown how contemplation of the universe is an unrestricted spiritual activity. However, this world also contains unseen beings and phenomena that provoke the curiosity of Muslims and form essential aspects of their faith. The question as to whether the contemplation of these unseen phenomena is also free from any restriction will be examined in the following chapter.

CHAPTER SIX

Contemplation of the Invisible and its Limits

Though Islamic contemplation is a free form of worship as there are no limitations to what a human being can experience or imagine – whether it is visible like the sun, the rivers and the planets, or invisible, like the angels and jinns – there is, nevertheless, one restriction, namely, the contemplation of the Divine Being Himself. Not only is it forbidden, but it is also impossible since none but God Himself knows what He really is. The Almighty says about Himself in the Qur'an: "He is the Creator of the heavens and the earth…There is nothing whatever like Him, and He is the One Who hears and sees [all things]" (42:11).

Moreover, God is free from the limits of time and space that confine humankind. Indeed, human beings cannot visualize an event without reference to a certain time and place, nor can they visualize anything without reference to a previous experience of their own. Try, for instance, to imagine a new type of animal, unlike any animal you know. Or try to imagine a color different from the colors you have already seen. No matter how hard you try, you will not be able to imagine that animal without drawing on what you know of animals: you may give it wings and attach them to its head, or attach ears onto its legs, yet the wings, the ears and the legs are all parts of animal bodies you already know. Furthermore, human beings can only hear within certain waves and vibrations – in which respect they are surpassed by many other animals and birds.

As previously stated, people still know very little about the brain and the nervous system that characterize them as human beings. The knowledge about their minds, souls and psyches are hidden secrets and protected treasures. If these are the limits of human beings in this transient world, then how can they have the audacity to presume that they could ever contemplate He Whom "no vision can grasp, but His grasp is over all vision" (6:103), He Who is not limited by time, since He is the One Who created time? Ibn Masʿūd said: "For your Lord, there is no night nor day. The light of heaven and earth derive from the light of His face...When He sits in judgment on the Last Day, the earth will shine with His light."[1] Scholars also affirm that whatever one imagines about the Divine Being, He is totally different from that. Ibn ʿAbbās said: "Some people tried to contemplate the Almighty, but the Prophet said to them: 'Contemplate the creation of God and not God Himself, for you can never give Him His due.'"[2] Al-Ghazālī wrote a poem that explains this point beautifully:

Tell those who can conceive my words:
Be brief; the answer is so long.
A hidden mystery there lies
Beyond the reach of the best of minds.
Where is the essence of the soul?
Can you behold it, or know how it roams?
The breaths, can you enumerate them?
No! You shall miss them all.
And where lies the mind? Where lie the cares
When you are overcome by sleep? Tell me, you ignorant!
The bread you eat, you know not how,
Nor how the urine passes through you!
If you fail so much to comprehend
Organs which your body holds,
How can you grasp the One, firm on the throne?
Ask not how the Word was revealed,
How the Lord speaks, or how He sees.
My word, this is but superfluous!
He has no 'where' nor 'how'
But He is Lord of 'how'
And He knows how the 'how' changes.
He, the Sublime in Attributes and Being
And Higher than all which you may say.[3]

The Attributes of God are of the same nature as His Being. Since the reality of the Divine Being can be known and understood only by Him, so can His Divine Attributes. However, believers can appreciate the beauty of these Attributes and this will guide them to the Divine Being in accordance with the level of their belief. Ibn ʿAbbās said:

> The Divine Being is shaded by His glorious Attributes and His Attributes are shaded by His deeds. So how do you feel about a Divine beauty shaded by Attributes of perfection, and adorned with epithets of grandeur and splendor?[4]

If Muslims are not allowed to contemplate the Divine Being, since they cannot grasp His sublime existence with their human senses and mind, then why are they encouraged to contemplate death, the barrier (*barzakh*) and the hereafter, all of which are invisible phenomena and inconceivable by our worldly means? The answer to this question is that although all these phenomena may have qualities inaccessible to the believers' minds in this world, they are in fact part of God's creation. They also have similitudes in this world. For instance, whoever experiences the mysteries of sleep, its nightmares and pleasant dreams, may be able to visualize death, the grave and the barrier. And whoever contemplates the lives of human beings in the darkness of the embryonic stage, and compares it with their lives after birth and in adulthood, may be able to visualize the vastness of what they will experience after they are freed by death from the material chains of this world. If a fetus in its mother's womb could be told about the world with its sun, moon, rivers, trees and fruits, it would not be able to visualize them because its experience is limited to its dark world. There, it does not need to eat, drink or breathe, since all the nourishment it needs is provided by the placenta or comes through the umbilical cord – which are the most important organs for its life. Indeed, they provide the fetus with 'ready-made' liquid nutrients and oxygen from the mother, and takes away the carbon dioxide and other wastes. Then, when the birth takes place and the fetus comes out into our world, the umbilical cord is severed and the placenta, which will have completed its duty, is buried or disposed of in some other way. No one will care about it, nor will any poet recite an elegy over its grave!

Our world is like a large womb, where the body plays the same role as the placenta in the womb. When the hour of death comes, the soul moves into a higher dimension of life in the barrier, which is so much larger and more complex than this world that it no longer needs the body (in the same way that the newborn no longer needs its placenta), and the body is buried. Thus, human beings keep moving from one stage into a higher one like a rocket, part of which, at the end of every stage and the consumption of its fuel, separates from its main body to make it go faster, with a lighter weight and a greater energy. This reminds us of the phrase, "Living people are asleep; they wake up when they die," and of the Arab saying: "Wakeful living is a slumber; death is waking; and man, between them, is a moving shadow."

Al-Ghazālī in his *Iḥyā' ʿUlūm al-Dīn* uses this image of the fetus in the womb to compare life in this world, life after death and life in the hereafter in a very impressive narrative which provokes contemplation in the unseen vastness of our future life in the next world. He writes:

> Man has two births: one is his "proceeding from between the backbone and the ribs" [the bodies of his father and mother] to the custody of the womb, where he is "in a place of rest, firmly fixed, for a period determined." Then he follows in the path of perfection from a drop of sperm, to a clot, then into a morsel of flesh. The second birth is when he proceeds from the narrow womb into the wider world. The ratio of the greater resurrection to the lesser one is like that of the wide world to the narrow womb. The ratio of the wide world of the hereafter to the transient world is like that of the wide world to the narrow womb, even wider and greater.[5]

Similarly, the bliss of paradise and all its fruits, flowing springs and beauties, have their similitude in our present world, although, of course, they are but trifles in comparison with what is offered in paradise. The Prophet is quoted to have said in a *ḥadīth qudsī:* "The Almighty said: 'I have prepared for my virtuous servants (a paradise) that no eye has seen, no ear has heard and no human mind has ever thought of.'"[6] Nevertheless, the similitude between the bliss of the transient world and that of the hereafter is revealing. The Qur'an declares that when the happy believers are admitted to paradise, they will be delighted to find fruits similar to what they ate in their former lives, only they will be finer and much more delectable. Their spouses will also be much more beautiful and pleasing in their companionship:

> Give glad tidings to those who believe and do righteous deeds that their portion shall be gardens beneath which rivers flow. Whenever they are granted fruits therefrom they will say: "Why, this is what was granted to us as sustenance before!" – for they shall be given things in similitude. And they shall have companions pure and holy, and they shall abide therein forever. (2:25)

This similarity thus confirms the ability of the Muslim to contemplate the pleasures of the hereafter in spite of the fact that their reality is beyond human comprehension. The same may be said of torment in hell. In this world, fire burns bodies and distorts faces. It is perhaps the severest torment imaginable in this world, which is why many worshippers shudder at the sight of flames, as they remind them of the fire in hell. Aḥmad ibn Ḥanbal, in his *Kitāb al-Zuhd* (The Book of Asceticism), relates that Ibn Masʿūd and al-Rabīʿ ibn Khaytham were once on the bank of the Euphrates. When al-Rabīʿ saw the blacksmiths heating ironware in their forge fire, the flaming blaze reminded him of hellfire, and he was so frightened that he collapsed unconscious. Ibn Masʿūd had to carry him home, where he lay unconscious from noon until the dawn of the following day.[7] Though his emotional reaction was too much for his psychological endurance, his condition was initiated by a cognitive associative memory in which he did not intend to lose touch with reality. The whole episode clearly demonstrates that it is possible for the believer to contemplate hellfire, despite its great difference from fire in this world. The Prophet described the inferno of the hereafter in the following words:

> Hell was fuelled for a thousand years until it turned red; then it was fueled for another thousand years until it turned white; then it was further fueled for a thousand years until it turned pitch black.[8]

In a related statement, Ibn ʿAbbās is reported to have said: "If one drop of the infernal tree, Zaqqūm, were tossed onto this world, it would ruin the life resources of all its inhabitants."[9]

Many early and modern scholars and worshippers have recorded their moving experiences of meditating on the nature of death, the barrier and the hereafter. Among these is al-Ḥārith al-Muḥāsibī who compiled the *Kitāb al-Tawahhum* (The Book of Imagination) in which he describes the tribulations of death, the bliss of paradise and the torment of hell. He moves readers to a visualization and contemplation of these transcendental images, describing them so minutely and effectively that readers can imagine themselves actually experiencing these colossal events. Here is how he describes the tribulations of death and resurrection:

> You imagine yourself beaten by death, unable to rise until the Day of Judgment when you have to appear before your Lord. You imagine yourself in the various tribulations of death, as the angel begins to pull your soul out of your feet, suffering tremendous pain therein. Then the angel turns to withdrawing the soul from the entire body, and your soul trickles upward through your body. The throes of death are now over all your body...Then you look at the face of the angel...and see him extending his hand to your mouth, to pull your soul out of your body, and you are overwhelmed by the sight...Then your heart pounds vigorously in suspense as you await the imminent Divine verdict: "Rejoice, you follower of God! You have gained His pleasure and reward" or "Woe to you, enemy of God! You have incurred His anger and punishment."
>
> When preparations of the dead are completed, and heaven and earth are emptied of their inhabitants who have quietened down after their agitation, nothing is heard and no one is seen except the Supreme Almighty, alone in Grandeur and Majesty, as He has always been. Then your soul is startled by a call to all creatures. You imagine the sound of that voice in your ears and your mind; then you realize that you are being called to appear before the Archangel. So your heart fails and your hair turns grey at the sound of that call. While you are so disturbed, you hear the earth opening above your head, so you jump to your feet, covered with the dust of your grave, staring toward the source of the sound,

with all other creatures roused with you, covered with the dust of the earth upon which they had suffered. You imagine their agitation and terror...You imagine your nakedness and disgrace...your cares and worries amid the crowding creatures, naked, barefooted and all silent in disgrace, fear and horror. You hear nothing but the shuffling of their feet...Sovereignty is stripped from the kings of the earth. They are humbled and disgraced more than any in the crowd, after their tyranny over the servants of God in His land. When the entire population of the earth is gathered together, including humans and jinn, devils and beasts, wild animals, cattle and flies, all in line, ready for judgment, the stars above them are scattered, the sun and the moon are eclipsed and the earth is darkened with the fading of its light. While you and the other creatures are aghast, the sky above spins, and you witness that horror, then it splits asunder, five hundred years deep...And lo! The clash in your ears! Then the sky crumbles into fragments, with the angels waiting on its sides to witness the Lord melting it into liquid silver, turning pale for fear of the Day of Judgment, as described by the Almighty: "It becomes red like ointment" (55:37).

Then the books start to fly right and left, and the scales are set up, and you imagine the scales set upright, while your heart anxiously follows to see where your book settles: on your right or on your left...While you wait with the other creatures you behold the Archangel ordering the myrmidons to step in. They approach with iron shovels and forks...You see them and your heart is overwhelmed with terror. Meanwhile your name is called in the presence of all: where is so-and-so? Imagine yourself shivering with terror...Imagine their grasping your arms in their rough hands as they drag you, gripping you tightly...until you are brought to the throne of the Compassionate, where they hurl you down. The Almighty Himself in His infinite greatness addresses you with His notable words: "Come closer, you son of Adam." You are lost in His light, as you are placed before the great Lord, Majestic and Generous. Your heart is laden with sorrow...and you look like a newborn lamb...How ashamed and frightened you are before the Lord Who has always been kind and protective towards you. So how will you answer when He asks you about your evil deeds and gross crimes?[10]

What al-Muḥāsibī recorded is a Muslim scholar's contemplation of the unseen affairs of death and the hereafter. It may be useful to quote a comparable contemplative statement from Sayyid Quṭb who has written extensively about the Day of Resurrection. The following commentary is about the opening verses of *Sūrah al-Takwīr*:

> When the sun is darkened; when the stars fall and disperse; when the mountains are made to move away; when camels, ten months pregnant, are left untended; when the wild beasts are brought together; when the seas are set alight; when men's souls are paired (like with like); when the infant girl, buried alive, is asked for what crime she was slain; when the records are laid open; when the sky is stripped bare; when Hell is made to burn fiercely; when Paradise is brought near – every soul shall know what it has put forward. (81:1–14)

> These verses sketch a scene of a great upheaval which envelops the whole universe. It is an event which reveals every guarded secret and leaves nothing hidden away. Every human being faces what he has put forward for the day of reckoning and judgement.
>
> The great events mentioned indicate that the present familiar state of the universe, with its perfect harmony, measured movement, controlled relations, perfected by a meticulous and able Maker will suffer a breakdown of its system. It will have completed its role. Along with all creation, it will move into a new predetermined phase of life, unlike anything known to us in this world.
>
> The *surah* aims to get this idea of the inevitable upheaval well established in men's hearts and minds so that they may attach little or no importance to the values and riches of this world, though these may seem to be of lasting consequence. The hearts and minds of people should establish a firm bond with the everlasting truth, i.e. the truth of God the Eternal, Who never changes when everything else changes and disappears. They should break the chains of what is familiar in this life in order to recognize the absolute truth which admits no restrictions of time, place, finite faculties or temporal standards.
>
> As one goes through the events of this universal upheaval, one cannot fail to observe an inner feeling for this affirmation.

As to what exactly happens to all these types of creation during the Resurrection we can only say that it is known to Allah alone. We can only comprehend what we have experienced. When we think of a great upheaval in the world our imagination cannot stretch beyond a violent earthquake or volcano, or, perhaps, the fall of a bomb. Floods are perhaps the most destructive manifestation of the power of water known to us. The most powerful events in the universe we have monitored were some limited explosions in the sun, which is millions of miles away from us. All these events, great as they may be, seem so small when they are compared to that universal upheaval which will take place on the Day of Resurrection that they may be considered akin to children's play. If we really want to know what will happen then, we can do no more than attempt to draw some sort of comparison with what we have experienced in this life.

The darkening of the sun probably means that it will cool down and its flames which stretch out for thousands of miles in space will dwindle and die down. As the sun is now in gas form because of its intense heat, which reaches a maximum of 12,000 degrees, its darkening probably means its transformation by freezing to a form similar to that of the surface of the earth. It may adopt a circular shape without becoming stretched out.

This is probably the meaning of the opening verse, but it could also mean something different. As to how it will happen, or what will cause it to happen, we can only say that this is known only to Allah.

The falling of the stars probably means that they will break away from the system which holds them together and lose their light and brightness. Only Allah knows which stars will be affected by this event: will it affect only a small group of stars, say, our own solar system, or our galaxy, which comprises hundreds of millions of stars, or will it affect all the stars in their millions of millions? It is a well-known fact that the universe comprises an almost infinite number of galaxies, each with its own space.

The forcing away of the mountains probably means that they will be crushed and blown away as indicated in other *surahs*: "*They ask you about the mountains. Say: 'My Lord will crush them to fine dust and leave them a desolate waste'*" (20:105). "*When the mountains crumble away and scatter into fine dust"* (56:5). *"And the mountains shall pass away as if they were a mirage"* (78:20). All these verses refer to a certain event which will affect the mountains and do away with their firm foundation and stability. This may be the beginning of the quake which will shake the earth violently, and which is mentioned in surah 99 "The Earthquake". *"When the earth is rocked in her last convulsion, when the earth shakes off her burdens"* (99:1–2). All these events will take place on that very long day.

"When the camels, ten months pregnant, are left untended." The Arabic description of the camel here specifies that she is in her tenth month of pregnancy. When in this state, she is to the Arab his most valuable possession because she is about to add to his wealth by a highly valued young camel, and to give him a lot of milk which he and his family will share with the new born animal. However, on that day, which will witness such overwhelming events, such priceless camels will be left without care, completely untended. The Arabs who were the first to be addressed by this verse never left such camels untended, except for the gravest of dangers.

"When the wild beasts are brought together." The great terror which overwhelms the wild beasts in their jungles is the cause of their coming together. They forget their mutual enmities, and move together, unaware of their direction. They neither seek their homes nor chase their prey as they usually do. The overwhelming terror changes the character of even the wildest of beasts. What would it do to man?

"When the seas are set alight." The Arabic term used here may mean that the seas will be over-filled with water, from floods similar to those which characterised the early stages of life on earth. On the other hand, earthquakes and volcanoes may remove the barriers now separating the seas so that the water of one will flow into the other. The Arabic expression may also mean that the seas will experience explosions which set them ablaze, as mentioned elsewhere in the Qur'an: *"When the oceans are made to explode"* (82:3). The explosions may result from separating the oxygen and the hydrogen which make the sea water. They could also be atomic explosions of some sort. If the explosion of a limited number of atoms in a hydrogen or atom bomb produces such dreadful consequences as we have seen, then the atomic explosion of the waters

of the oceans, in whatever manner it may occur, will produce something much too fearful for our minds to visualise. Similarly, we cannot conceive the reality of Hell, which stands beyond these vast oceans.

"*When men's souls are paired (like with like).*" The pairing of souls may mean the reunion of body and soul at the time of resurrection. It may also mean their grouping, like with like, as mentioned elsewhere in the Qur'an: "*You will be divided into three groups*" (56:7) – the chosen elite, the people of the right, and the people of the left. It may also mean some other way of grouping.[11]

This should be enough to clarify the importance of contemplation and free meditation on whatever objects throughout the universe, unimpeded by the limitations of time and place in this world or those of the hereafter. Nothing exists in this universe save God the Creator and His creation. Believers are prohibited from contemplating the Divine Being, but they are free to contemplate everything else.

CHAPTER SEVEN

Individual Levels of Contemplation

Are there different degrees of contemplation and meditation and, if so, is the level of contemplation reached proportionate to the effort made by the contemplator? Are there differences between individuals in this respect? And are some objects easier to contemplate than others? To answer these questions fully is beyond the power of the human mind. Nevertheless, there are at least nine dimensions and variables that seem to interrelate in the formation of these differences. These will now be examined.

DEPTH OF FAITH

The depth of contemplation and meditation depends, before anything else, on the level of faith of the individuals and their closeness to God. The stronger the faith, the easier it is for them to contemplate God's domain and to invoke thereof the noblest feelings of love and appreciation of their Creator. However, this is a subjective matter, which is known only to God and the believers themselves.

As mentioned earlier, contemplation passes through various stages: the initial perceptual-cognitive stage; the stage of appreciation of the precision and beauty of creation; and the stage when this appreciation is extended to the Creator Himself. Hence, the greater the individual's faith, love and veneration of God, the deeper their contemplation of and meditation on the creation of the heavens and the earth. If believers continue to contemplate and meditate while they are in this warm spiritual and emotional state, they will move from the cold cognitive stage to between the second and third stages, where they can be described as moving between cognition and contemplation. This can lead to an intense emotional state of ecstasy that may at times be too strong for their psychological system to bear.

One can read curious stories about the genuine contemplation of worshippers. Indeed, a person may start contemplating in a calm state, but then becomes so lost in thought that he or she is unaware of their surroundings. For instance, it is reported by al-Ghazālī in *Iḥyā' ᶜUlūm al-Dīn* that Dāūd al-Ṭāᶜī climbed onto the roof of his house on the night of a full moon to contemplate the grandeur of heaven and earth. However, he became so engaged in his meditation, looking at the sky and weeping, that he fell into his neighbor's house. The neighbor jumped out of bed, sword in hand, thinking he was a thief. When he recognized Dāūd, he put down his sword and asked him who had pushed him off his own roof. Dāūd replied: "By God, I was never aware of that."[1]

DEPTH AND LENGTH OF CONCENTRATION

The second factor is related to the personality of the believers and their innate ability to concentrate without becoming tired or bored quickly. This quality depends mostly on the nature of the nervous system with which they were granted by the Almighty. A number of experimental research studies were carried out and show clear differences in people's ability to concentrate with patience. Some of these psychological studies were conducted on extroverts and introverts, and showed that the power of concentration has a biological basis in the human nervous system, and that it lies in the reticular formation and activating system. This formation, which is situated at the stem of the brain, acts as a gate controlling the nervous pulses and stimuli which go up to the higher centers of the brain.

In introverts, the reticular formation magnifies the nervous signals sent by the various sense organs to the brain. As a result, these people have a greater ability to concentrate and can do so for a longer period of time. Such individuals are content with the least sensory stimulation in their environment; consequently, they tend to prefer solitude and are introspective. They generally cannot tolerate loud voices or high-pitched music, and do not like very bright colors. They prefer activities which do not require them to mix with people and participate in exciting activities, such as reading alone, or working in the garden, or in the library. They enjoy their routine work without getting bored, and tend to be careful in planning their life affairs. In their social relations they are reticent, not revealing their secrets except to very few of their closest friends. They rarely show explosive emotions, or react in a hostile, angry, or spontaneous manner. The results of many experiments have confirmed that introverts can do work which demands continuous concentration for long periods, with only a narrow margin of error caused by inhibition and fatigue. We can therefore expect this type of people to be able to engage in deep cognitive activities for a comparatively long time. And if they are also meditative believers, they can engage in deep contemplation on the creation longer and more deeply than other people.

On the other hand, extroverts have a nervous system whose reticular formation inhibits or weakens the nervous signals and stimuli that go to the upper centers of the brain. Consequently, and contrary to the previous type, such people need intense and exciting experiences in their environment to substitute for the inhibition of their nervous reticular formation – at least this is what the supporters of this theory claim. They like public gatherings, and enjoy having a large number of friends, because they are in great need of stimulation, a change of scenery, and constant conversation. They dislike loneliness, are averse to reading, and are impatient with routine activities. They often move house, and change jobs, food, friends, and even spouses. They do not hide their feelings, and they can be violent. They are quick-tempered, but forgive quickly, and they prefer work that does not demand continuous concentration, or is repetitive. Laboratory experiments have also shown that extroverts make more mistakes and that they concentrate less than introverts in various mental and physical activities.[2] If this is true, by virtue of their nervous constitution, these people may be less patient than others when it comes to deep and lengthy thinking and cognitive activities, though their faith and commitment may be similar.

Even if we accept the fact that introverts are on a higher level than extroverts in the sphere of contemplation, this does not automatically mean that extroverts are of a lower standing. Indeed, by virtue of their nervous and psychological system, they may surpass the introverts in Islamic endeavors that demand mixing with people and making friends or speaking in public. In any case, most people are somewhere between introvert and extrovert, the numbers gradually decreasing toward either extreme.

EMOTIONAL AND MENTAL STATE OF THE CONTEMPLATOR

The third factor that affects the depth of contemplation is a psychological one. Indeed, contemplation requires peace of mind and tranquillity, as well as both psychological and physical health. Physical health is without doubt essential for enhancing the depth of contemplation. Indeed, it is obvious that the sick person, the overeating obese individual, or the one suffering from drug addiction cannot elevate his spiritual status to a high level of contemplation. As I have already discussed the great benefits to physical health from following the Islamic way of life in my book *The AIDS Crisis: An Islamic Socio-Cultural Perspective*, I will devote this section to the influence of the psychological aspects.[3]

The believer who is afflicted with anxiety, depression, obsession, hypochondria or any other psychological disorder cannot be expected to contemplate with a high degree of concentration. Neurotics may be able to meditate on a low level, but those afflicted with psychosis, mental derangement, severe mental retardation or senility may not even be able to do that. Thus, between tranquil normality and severe psychosis there are degrees of psychological and emotional states that affect the ability to contemplate in proportion with the severity of each case.

Undoubtedly, for the contemplative believer, the psychological malady is more of a burden than the physical malady. In fact, many worshippers welcome physical maladies, since they claim that such illnesses may become an opportunity for deeper meditation and contemplation and more spiritually motivated worshipping and remembrance. On the other hand, worry, anxiety, depression and a heavy heart are all enemies to the tranquillity needed by believers in their contemplation: hence, the Prophet's prayer in which he asks God to protect him from anxiety, sadness, weakness and laziness.[4] We find in our psychiatric and clinical psychological practice that these emotional states from which the Prophet asked God to save him are, in fact, the main symptoms of states of anxiety and depression.

ENVIRONMENTAL FACTORS

The fourth factor is the effect of the environment on believers, and concerns how they deal with the needs and problems of everyday life, and the extent to which these needs can impede or enhance their ability to contemplate. For instance, a Muslim man who has a kind and dutiful wife, who teaches Qur'anic interpretation at university several hours a week, and who lives in a country where all the requirements of comfortable living are provided will find that everything in his environment encourages perseverance in contemplation and meditation. In contrast, a believer who has to work for long strenuous hours in some private corporation, spending most of his time in commercial accounting and government tenders, then finishes his tiring work to stand in long queues before bakeries and gas-stations to provide the necessities of living for himself and his dissatisfied family will certainly not find the time or the tranquillity for profound contemplation – even though he may be equal to the other person in his faith, and similar to him in his nervous and psychological disposition.

INFLUENCE OF CULTURE

The child-rearing practices of some cultures, whether they are Islamic or not, inculcate in their people, from early childhood, the love and appreciation of natural and artificial artistic beauty. Adults who grew up in such cultures then spend much of their time and money to enjoy and contemplate a picturesque landscape or buy a beautiful painting. On the other hand, there are cultures that bring up their people to be attracted by very little beyond the physical beauty of women and maybe the appreciation of poetry and local music.

It is sad that many of our Muslim societies fit into the second category. I remember very vividly, in the 1930s, seeing English men and women driving their own cars or hiring taxis or cycling in the hot weather to the White Nile Bridge of Khartoum to watch the sunset. Indeed, the sunset in Khartoum is an extraordinary natural phenomenon. Khartoum marks the spot where the White Nile, with its chalky water, meets the Blue Nile carrying the silt of black soil. The two swift rivers confront each other with a clear dividing line preventing the mixture of the bluish and whitish waters, as though they are a white wrestler and a black wrestler locked in a conflict of equal strength. The sun sets with a deep red-orange hue widely permeating the vastness of the western blue sky which is browned by the dusty desert of Omdurman. These English 'appreciaters' were not tourists, but simply settlers colonizing the Sudan. A number of them made a daily excursion to the White Nile Bridge, and I remember how Sudanese onlookers and taxi drivers would wonder at the vain behavior of these Westerners: "What do they see in a setting sun?" and comment ironically "They have so much money that they don't know how to spend wisely!"

In such cultures, the few people who somehow have a talent for appreciating natural beauty and can spend time meditating on it, may often appear rather eccentric to their compatriots. In this connection, the reader may be amused to hear an anecdote about one such refined person, who was a cousin of mine who lived in our little town, Rufa'a, on the Blue Nile. One day, he packed his suitcase to travel to the capital, Khartoum and, as he was waiting for the train, which generally arrives late, he saw a very attractively colored bird, unlike the birds of that part of the Sudan, perched on the telephone line. He was so impressed with its beauty that he followed it as it gracefully flew from one spot on the line to another. When it finally flew away, he came back to where he had been waiting only to find that somebody had stolen his suitcase. Though this incident happened in the 1960s, to this day my relatives in Rufa'a still laugh about it and recall it as evidence for his absorption with 'trivialities'.

Thus one would expect believers who come from a culture that encourages the appreciation of natural beauty to be better contemplators than those coming from cultures that do not bring up their children to admire the aesthetic aspects of life. It is this latter group which the Qur'an addresses when it speaks about the beauty of

God's creation and the different colors and hues in people, animals and rocks.

BELIEVERS' KNOWLEDGE OF THE SUBJECTS OF CONTEMPLATION

The sixth factor depends on how far people are acquainted with and have knowledge of the objects of their contemplation, because they will more easily choose and appreciate objects of meditation that are in their familiar surroundings. For instance, whereas I may look at the sky and meditate on its charming beauty, its spaciousness and its twinkling stars, believers who are experts in astronomy will look at the sky and meditate on what their eyes can and cannot see. They see in the scattered sparkling stars billions of flaming suns which hurl their fires into the space beyond; they see millions of constellations that are millions of light-years away, travelling away from one another at formidable speeds of up to 40,000 miles per second. Such scientists look at the sky and truly appreciate that the universe is progressively expanding, and can thus understand the verse of the Qur'an, "We have built the heavens with might and indeed We shall make them wider" (51:47). They also feel the oneness of God in the unity of His creation. They see this unity in the electrons, protons and other sub-atomic particles that constitute the building blocks of everything in this universe. They even see it through the vision of Einstein's theory in which space and time have been united in one physical feature while mass and energy have become two facets of the same electromagnetic phenomenon. Even if we were on the same level of faith, concentration and presence of heart as the astronomers, they would still reach a much higher level of contemplation than ourselves owing to their deeper and wider knowledge.

In the following passage from *The Tao of Physics*, Fritjof Capra describes a deep contemplative experience aided by his knowledge as a physicist:

> I was sitting by the ocean one late summer afternoon, watching the waves rolling in and feeling the rhythm of my breathing, when I suddenly became aware of my whole environment as being engaged in a

> gigantic cosmic dance. Being a physicist, I knew that the sand, rocks, water and air around me were made of vibrating molecules and atoms, and that these consisted of particles which interacted with one another by creating and destroying other particles...All this was familiar to me from my research in high-energy physics, but until that moment I had only experienced it through graphs...and mathematical theories. As I sat on that beach, my former experience came to life; I 'saw' cascades of energy coming down from outer space...I 'saw' the atoms of the elements and those of my body participating in this cosmic dance...I felt its rhythm and I heard its sound.[5]

GOOD EXAMPLE AND INFLUENCE OF COMPANIONSHIP

The Prophet said, "A man is the like of his companion, so be careful whom you befriend."[6] The influence of good example and companionship needs no elaboration. Religion has explained it, observations by average people have affirmed it, and modern experimental social psychology has confirmed it, to the extent that it has become a foregone conclusion. In the same way that bad example is a great handicap, good example and companionship make one of the most important factors affecting the profundity of the believer's contemplation. It is for this reason that a disciple or *murīd* can benefit much from his association and identification with a worshipper who has reached the level of the tranquil soul (*al-nafs al-mutma'innah*) in the person of his spiritual master (shaykh). Indeed, the spiritual influence of the companionship of a sage can dramatically change the worldview of his disciple and increase his Islamic meditative ability.

As we have explained earlier, sound contemplation covers all human cognitive and emotional fields, and it becomes deeper and more transcendent with perseverance and when it is combined with the mention and glorification of God, until believers reach a level where they perceive God's power, wisdom, mercy, and all His other qualities in everything they see and hear around them. Describing this state, Ibn al-Qayyim says in *Madārij al-Sālikīn* that the worshipper's deep and continuous contemplation will open for him a divine gate through which he will:

> ...look up at the Most High and Supreme, as if he can see and behold Him above His heavens, resting on His Throne, observing His creation, hearing their voices, seeing their inner intents. Then the gate of eternity is opened before the worshipper, and through it he sees that all the cosmic changes and affairs of existence are in the hands of the Almighty alone. Then, when he beholds any of the Almighty's creation, it will demonstrate for him the Almighty Creator, His Attributes of perfection and qualities of majesty. None of His creation will veil the worshipper from his Creator. Each element of the creation will address the worshipper, saying: "Listen to my testimony before Him Who created everything in the best mould. I am the work of God, Who created best..." When this happens, the worshipper has nothing of the universe left in his heart except God, the Supreme. The lights of knowledge, truth, sincerity and love then flow from his heart as the light flows from the sun.[7]

There is no doubt that this light, which Ibn al-Qayyim likens to sunlight, also flows to anyone who meets such worshippers, befriends them, or becomes their disciple.

NATURE OF THE OBJECTS OF CONTEMPLATION

The eighth factor that affects depth of contemplation is the nature of the object of contemplation and meditation. I have already explained the ease with which people can contemplate the natural creation, such as the mountains, the rivers and the forests, in comparison with thinking of human inventions and relating them to the grace of God. The reason for this is that inventions need a greater degree of abstraction than natural things. Moreover, some natural phenomena immediately stimulate thought and strong feelings, shaking the psychological and spiritual aspects of human beings to the core, and imposing themselves on their hearts and minds. For instance, the dazzling flash of lightning, the deafening rumble of thunder, the heavy downpour of rain, or the roaring of the wind – all have a definite impact on the human soul and can easily lead to effortless contemplation connected with fear of God and hope for His mercy. The Qur'an proclaims: "It is He Who shows you the lightning, by way of both fear and hope. It is He Who raises up the clouds, heavy with fertilizing rain. Thunder repeats His praise and so do the angels with awe..." (13:12–13).

On the other hand, some phenomena are hard to contemplate, either because they are artificial such as human technological inventions or because they are extremely abstract. Because of their hypothetical and conceptual nature, they are beyond the limits of time and place, and it is difficult for the average human mind to visualize or comprehend them. Examples of these phenomena have already been given.

FAMILIARITY OF THE OBJECTS OF CONTEMPLATION

Although knowledge and understanding of the objects of contemplation can encourage deeper contemplation, it should not be surprising that the opposite is also true: namely, that extreme familiarity with the object can be a hindrance to contemplating it. Indeed, monotonous repetition drains the greatest cosmic phenomena of their grandeur and splendor. Otherwise, how can we not be moved by the sight of the sunrise every morning, with all the clear majestic signs that it carries? How can our souls not be filled with submissive love for God when we observe and make use of His creations all day long: plants, animals, birds and fish?

It is interesting to quote what Ibn al-Jawzī recorded about this issue of familiarity and novelty. He mentions how, during his long journey to Makkah for the pilgrimage, he was deeply touched by the sight of the huge mountains of the Khaybar, and reproached himself for experiencing such an intense feeling of submissive love and fearful appreciation of the Almighty only after contemplating those mountains. Then he started to remember the great seas, the skies and the stars that he had so often observed but failed to be so deeply moved by. This is how Ibn al-Jawzī described his experience:

> On my pilgrimage to Makkah, I was somewhat apprehensive of the Bedouin bandits, so I followed the Khaybar path. I saw such colossal mountains and wondrous paths which were amazing. The greatness of the Creator increased in my heart, the like of which I had never felt

before. I cried to my soul: "Shame on you! Cross to the sea and look at its wonders with the eye of the soul, and you shall witness even greater grandeur. Then observe the universe, and it will seem, in relation to the [seven] heavens and orbits, to be no more than a grain of sand in the desert. Then imagine the orbits and God's Throne, paradise and hell... Then leave all this and turn back to see that it is all in the grip of the Almighty Whose power knows no limits. After that, turn to yourself to see your beginning and your end. Think of what was before the beginning: it was but nothingness; and of what will be after the end, which is but ashes and dust. How can a person be at ease with this world, when the eye of his soul sees the beginning and the end? How can the sensitive at heart be inattentive to the remembrance of God? Upon my life, if human souls were to turn away from their fancies, they would melt from fear of God or swoon with love for Him. But the senses have been dulled so much that the power of the Creator can be realized only at the sight of a mountain. Yet, had they the wit to realize the true meaning of this, then the Power over that mountain would have been more indicative than the mountain itself."[8]

The greater our familiarity with our surroundings, the heavier the veil over our vision and awareness, and we fail to observe or remember very important things. In fact, it is possibly this veil of familiarity which has impeded people from contemplating the human being in flesh, blood and soul. Indeed, throughout the ages, people have been able to examine everything around them, and have developed their knowledge in geology, agriculture, chemistry, astronomy, transport, the means of production, the art of war, etc. Yet, though mankind has made great progress in the material and biological studies, human sciences like psychology and sociology are still lagging considerably behind. Although this is to some extent because these social sciences totally disregarded the soul and the spiritual aspects of human beings, it is also because they foolishly mimicked the methodologies used by the physical sciences and that their study began very late in comparison with the physical and biological sciences.

This chapter has so far examined some of the most important factors that can affect depth of contemplation, and thus led to an interactive discussion of the intellectual, psychological and spiritual aspects of the Muslim believer. The next step is to assess the relative importance of these factors.

Undoubtedly, the importance of any of these factors depends on the circumstances of the contemplators themselves. In some cases, contemplation deepens considerably if believers are in a better psychological and emotional state. In other cases, Muslims will find it easier to meditate constantly if they move away from the noisy city to a remote and quiet village. Nevertheless, the basic factor in the depth of contemplation is that of faith. Depth of faith and nearness to God are the backbone of contemplation; the other elements are secondary factors that derive their influence from the strength of that faith. Modern scholars, particularly those designated as the neo-Muʿtazilites, are far from the truth when they claim that we are nowadays more capable than our forefathers – even than the Companions of the Prophet – to contemplate God's creation simply because we know more about the nature of things as a result of the great advances achieved in modern science and technology. Indeed, the real effect of what believers see and feel in their environment depends much more on the depth of their faith and their submissive love of God than on what they know and discover about the nature of things. Contemplation is a warm emotional state where believers are affected by what they feel and grasp of the precision and beauty in God's vast universe; it is not a cold fact-finding state enhanced by the increase of knowledge.

A conceptual, though simplistic, illustration can be given if one imagines that these parameters are measurable by identical units that increase or decrease according to the circumstances of the contemplating Muslim. If we give the Faith factor the symbol 'F', the ability to Concentrate the symbol 'C', the believer's Knowledge of the object under contemplation the symbol 'K', the Qualities of the object under contemplation the symbol 'Q', and so on, then the depth of contemplation will depend on the influence of the Faith factor 'F' on each of the other parameters. This may be put in a simplistic equation as follows:

$$\text{Depth of Contemplation} = F\,(C+K+Q+\ldots)$$

This equation shows that an increase in the faith factor will lead to a multiplication in the depth of contemplation, for it interacts with all the other factors. However, when the other factors increase, they will have only a limited additive effect on the depth of contemplation, which is like the difference between adding figures and multiplying them. Similarly, when the faith factor 'F' falls to zero, which corresponds to total disbelief, the other factors will be worthless, no matter how large in size, because the result of multiplying any figure by zero is no more than zero. Therefore, those who have a degree of faith like that of the Companions of the Prophet will need little knowledge of what they see in their environment and much less time in order to achieve depths of contemplation that are far beyond the reach of weaker people. In figures, if a Muslim has a weak faith of 10 units but has extensive knowledge about the object of his contemplation, has all the time and peace of mind he needs, and other factors, which add up to 100, then his depth of contemplation will be 1,000 units. However, someone who has much less knowledge and less time may secure only half the units of contemplation, that is 50, but since he possesses a high faith factor of 100 units, his depth of contemplation will reach 5,000 – namely, five times as much as the former! Naturally, spiritual and religious concepts such as faith and contemplation cannot be subjected to such simple and superficial measurements and equations – it is a mere notion that seemed interesting to share with readers in order to clarify the point that was being made.

I hope that readers who wish to improve their practice of this great form of worship and achieve deeper contemplation will benefit from the explanations given. They can explore their positive natural God-given abilities and their beneficial environmental and spiritual endowments in order to make full use of them in expanding the realm of their contemplation until it is deeply and habitually inculcated in their psychological and spiritual entity. They should also try to discover the factors and habits that deter them from contemplation in order to avoid them. If people are sincere and highly motivated, they will surely be guided to surmount all the obstacles to worshipping the Almighty and contemplating His creation. There is always a creative and unforeseen solution to chronic problems.

For example, a very busy friend of mine who used to complain of lack of time for meditation and remembrance of God suddenly discovered that he lost two hours every day in driving to and from work. Realizing this, and choosing to use the time he spent in his car to contemplate and remember God, not only enabled him to use his time more efficiently, but it also took away all the anxieties and tensions of a long drive and the provocation of road-bullies.

Although this chapter has examined the most important factors leading to individual differences among believers, it is obvious that each believer has his or her own circumstances and individual life experiences which have their own bearing on the entire process of contemplation.

CHAPTER EIGHT

Experimental Science and Religion: The Cosmic Laws

When one considers the high position given by Islam to the contemplation of God's creation, one realizes the woeful position of those whose hearts, ears, eyes and minds are closed to the distinct signs of God, even though these are displayed before them, day and night, throughout the universe.

> And how many signs in the heavens and the earth do they pass by? Yet they turn away from them. (12:105)

Some of these people may have knowledge of the signs of God through the laws they discover relating to matter, energy and biology, but this knowledge does not take them beyond the superficial external aspects, or transport them from the wonders of the creation to the Creator. The Qur'an describes them as follows:

> They know of the outer [superficial] things of this world; but of the hereafter they are heedless. (30:7)

In fact, this crossing from the observed physical, psychosocial and biological phenomena to the Creator marks the basic difference between the practice of non-Muslim experimental scientists and Muslim contemplation. Indeed, the early steps of contemplation that involve the contemplation of humankind's outer environment are based on conscious and close observation using the senses of hearing, sight, smell, taste and touch, and is a similar kind of observation to that used as an initial step in the scientific method. In experimental science, only empirical evidence based on observation is accepted; the results produced are then used for generalizations, hypotheses and applications. Similarly, to verify their hypotheses, the experimental scientists go back to a new phase of observation and examination. In his book *Human Behavior*, L. Malpass mentions how Alfred North Whitehead likens experimental science to an aeroplane which takes off from the solid ground of observation to fly into the thin air of generalizations and theories, only to land again on the ground of observation and perception through the senses.[1]

Another similarity between the Muslim's contemplation of the universe and the research of the experimental scientist is that in their initial observation, they are not looking for the diverse and unrelated detailed components of the objects of study, but for their general and more permanent aspects, such as the laws that govern their functions. The reason for this is that, irrespective of belief and by their very nature, human beings reject chaos and ambiguity, and tend to impose order and clarity on the countless stimuli with which they are continually faced. Even in the simple sensory perception of incomplete or vague forms, individuals in laboratory experiments were found to complete spontaneously the gaps or unclear parts in the figures in order to obtain the familiar form of a circle, a triangle or any other symbol like the flag of a certain country or the insignia of a certain association. This tendency of human beings to perceive sensory patterns as meaningful well-organized wholes rather than as disconnected parts is in fact the phenomenon which incited German psychologists to establish the psychological perspective known as the Gestalt – a German term that can be translated as the 'whole'.

The same phenomenon can be seen in how people apprehend what they perceive with other senses or through their higher mental processes, which they need for problem-solving, abstraction and concept-forming. For instance, when people look at the universe, they instinctively begin to search for the laws that govern its various phenomena in order to be able to anticipate their incidence within the orderliness of this framework and do away with the frustrating ambiguity.

What moves the heart of believers most are the secrets they learn about the Divine laws that govern God's creation, whether it is the discovery of the chemical language of a tiny ant or the discovery of the orbit of a huge planet. This innate nature, which God implanted in the hearts of all human beings, is perhaps the reason why some present-day scientists speak a similar language to that of worshippers. Here, for example, is what an American professor of biology, Cecil Hamann, says about the Baltimore bird:

> What about the nest of the Baltimore bird? Who taught this bird that fine art? Why do all nests built by these birds look alike? If you say it is the instinct, then that is one way out of the question; but it is an inadequate answer. What is an instinct? Some people say it is the behavior which the animal does *not* learn. Is it not logical, then, to see the power of God manifested in these creatures which He created according to laws of which we hardly know a thing about?[2]

When we read what the contemplative Muslim scholars have been writing, since the earliest generation of Islam, we can be easily astonished by their precise observations, especially when compared with what modern scientists have learned. For instance, following the theme of birds, al-Ghazālī recorded in *Al-Ḥikmah fī Makhlūqāt Allāh* his detailed contemplative observations of the intricate creation of birds in a manner similar to that of modern scientists:

> Know, may God bless you, that the Almighty created the bird and made it light to help it fly, with nothing heavy to weigh it down...He created feet for the bird but no hands, making the skin of the legs coarse and well wrought...for it might need to alight in places where there is water and mud...Were the legs covered with feathers, they would be harmed by wetness and dirt...all this helps the bird in its flight. He created the chest semi-circular, to make it easier to pass through the air...so are the rounded tips of the wings. The Almighty made the roots of the feathers firm, woven upright to suit the coarse skin on the wings...He protected the bird with these feathers against the heat and the cold, and provided the wings with the strongest feathers, where they are well fixed, for they are needed most, while the rest of the body is covered with a different kind of lighter feathers for warmth, protection and beauty...Then contemplate a single feather, and you will see that it is woven, like cloth,

> from thin threads, strong enough to hold together, and flexible enough so that it does not break. The feathers are hollow to make flight easier...and they are not affected by wet weather, and dirt does not soil them. When sprayed with water, the slightest shake will get rid of the moisture, and the bird will be light again. The Almighty gave the bird one outlet in the body, for laying eggs and excretion, to lessen its weight. He also made the bird lay eggs and not bear offspring, for that would make the bird too heavy in flight. He created the tail feathers to help the bird fly steadily, otherwise the wings would pull right and left during flight, thus, the tail acts like a rudder that steadies the movement of a ship.[3]

This example shows how deep, spiritually motivated meditation can bestow on such an ancient Muslim scholar the ability and knowledge to speak about the creation of the bird and its flight as if he were a modern specialist in aerodynamics. Birds are beautiful, graceful creatures that have always fascinated people by their ability to fly elegantly through the sky, to the extent that human beings tried to imitate the creation of the birds and finally achieved this ambition by inventing the aeroplane.

The next creatures to consider are tiny insects such as ants. The following is part of Muṣṭafā Maḥmūd's summary of the recent scientific studies on these amazing creatures:

> A moment's contemplation of one small ant is enough to cause great astonishment. How did this ant learn to build these complex geometrical houses, with their passageways, villages, warehouses and storage areas? How did the ant join in a community where specializations and functions are accurately assigned? How did it learn to catch other insects and herd them before it? The communication among these great numbers of ants in an organized community means that they have found some kind of a common language. The latest studies in this field show that the ants communicate among themselves, not through a spoken language or by signs, but through a chemical language. Observe an anthill. Every now and then, you will find two ants meeting and exchanging what look like kisses or whispers...In fact these are neither

kisses nor whispers, but each ant secretes in the other ant's mouth a special type of saliva with a chemical quality which means: "Let us do this or that..." There is another thing about the ants which we cannot call intellect, but looks more like insight...the ant stores up food, grains, crumbs and left-overs, then guards them against raiders in preparation for the winter which has not yet arrived...It does all this without having the ability to think or to imagine the future: its circumstances and needs. How does all this happen?[4]

If one compares this with the writings of contemplators of the early generations of Muslim scholars, one notices that the latter present accurate observations like that of present-day scholars. In *Nahj al-Balāghah*, ʿAlī ibn Abī Ṭālib said about the ant and the grasshopper:

Look at the ant with its small body and delicate form. It can hardly be seen in the corner of the eye, nor by the perception of the imagination – how it moves on the earth and leaps at its livelihood. It carries the grain to its hole and deposits it in its place of stay. It collects during the summer for its winter, and during strength for the period of its weakness. Its livelihood is guaranteed, and it is fed according to fitness. Allah, the Kind, does not forget it and (Allah the Giver) does not deprive it, even though it may be in the dry stone or fixed rocks.

If you have thought about its digestive tracts in its high and low parts, the carapace of its belly, and its eyes and its ears in its head you would be amazed at its creation and you would feel difficulty in describing it. Exalted is He who made it stand on its legs and erected it on its pillars (of limbs). No other originator took part with Him in its creation. If you tread the paths of your imagination and reach its extremity it will not lead you anywhere except to the Originator of the date-palm, because everything has (the same) delicacy and detail, and every living being has little difference.

In His creation, the big, the delicate, the heavy, the light, the strong, the weak are all equal. So is the sky, the air, the winds and the water. Therefore, you look at the sun, moon, vegetation, plants, water, stone, the difference of this night and day, the springing of the streams, the large number of mountains, the heights of their peaks, the diversity of languages and the variety of tongues. Then woe be to him who disbelieves in the Ordainer and denies the Ruler. They believe that they are like grass for which there is no cultivator nor any maker for their diverse shapes. They have not relied on any argument for what they assert, nor any research for what they have heard. Can there be any construction without a constructor, or any offence without an offender[?]

If you wish you can tell about the locust (as well). Allah gave it two red eyes, lighted for them two moon – like pupils, made for it small ears, opened for it a suitable mouth and gave it keen sense, gave it two teeth to cut with and two sickle-like feet to grip with. The farmers are afraid of it in the matter of crops since they cannot drive it away even though they may join together. The locust attacks the fields and satisfies its desires (of hunger) from them although its body is not equal to a thin finger.[5]

In a similar statement which reveals the depth of his contemplation and his astute observation, Ibn al-Qayyim wrote in *Miftāḥ Dār al-Saᶜādah*:

Think of this weak ant and its clever ways in gathering its food and storing it. You see signs and learn lessons in all that. Watch a group of ants going out to look for food. They work in two teams: one carries the food home, the other goes out searching for it. The two teams do not collide, but they look like two separate strings. If they find something too heavy to carry, a group of ants will come to help; then they divide the catch at the entrance of their house. Here is another amazing example of their cleverness: when they carry the grain to their holes, they break it into pieces to stop it from sprouting. If the grain has two halves that sprout, they will break the grain into four pieces. When the grain becomes damp, they take it outside to dry in the sun, then they take it in again. This is why you sometimes see a lot of broken grain near their holes, but you come back later to see that it is all gone.[6]

In his discussion on ants, Ibn al-Qayyim relates an interesting anecdote reported by a worshipper who was deeply interested in observing and contemplating ants and their activities. He carried out a scientific experiment which led him to conclude that ants have a special language of communication, and that they impose a rigorous punishment upon the one who brings wrong information and, in doing so, misleads the community of ants. Ibn al-Qayyim wrote:

> A worshipper related the following story to me: "I saw an ant finding a piece of a grasshopper and trying to haul it up but failing. Then it went away and came back with a group of ants to help. Before they arrived, I picked up the piece from the ground. When the ant and its companions returned, they all went in a circle around the place where the dead grasshopper was; but finding nothing, they went away. Then I put the slice back where it was, and the ant came back and tried to carry it away, but in vain. So, once again, it went to fetch some help, and, once again, I picked up the piece before they returned. When the group came back to find nothing, they encircled that ant, and before I could do anything to help it, they attacked it, tearing it to pieces, one limb after another, as I was watching in astonishment."[7]

In his *Tafsīr al-Kashshāf* (Interpretation of the Qur'an), the Muslim scholar, al-Zamakhsharī, described insects that are so small that they cannot be seen with the naked eye and, in doing so predicted the discovery of microscopic beings.

> You may have noticed inside the folds of old books a minute insect that can hardly be discerned with the sharp naked eye, except when it moves. When it stops moving it becomes invisible. If you move your hand towards it, it moves away to avoid any probable harm. Glory be to Him Who perceives the form of that insect: its organs, whether visible or not, the details of its creation, its eyesight, and hidden intentions! Perhaps there are beings extremely minute and infinitesimal in his creation. "Glory be to God, Who created in pairs all things that the earth produces as well as their own [human] kind, and things of which [they] have no knowledge" (36:36).[8]

In a state of profound spiritual transcendence, he then went on to say that this reminded him of a poem that he had composed. Its verses are very moving when read in Arabic. The translation is as follows:

O You Who see the mosquito
Extending its wings in the deep, dark night,
And see the heart veins in its neck,
And the marrow in those thin membranes,
Forgive a worshipper who now repents
His going astray in the olden times.[9]

Such scholars did not stop at contemplating visible creatures, but went on to meditate on abstract concepts, including the process of contemplation itself. Here is what al-Ghazālī wrote while contemplating the mind and the powers entrusted to it:

> The mind is not a person or an image that can be seen; it is not a sound that can be heard, nor can it be touched, smelt or tasted. Yet, it commands and is obeyed. It always seeks its growth. It can think of the invisible, and is capable of seeing it. What is too narrow for the eye is wide enough for it. What is too large for any vessel can be contained in it. It believes in matters veiled by the Almighty among and beyond His skies and beneath His earth. It can see all this more clearly than any eye can see. It is the site of wisdom and the essence of knowledge. The more knowledge it gains, the more spacious and powerful it becomes. It orders the limbs to move, but the time between the intention to obey and the action itself is too short to tell, though the readiness to move comes first.[10]

Al-Ghazālī went on to ponder over the wisdom of the Almighty in limiting the faculties of the mind in newborn babies. He spoke about mental development with the observational ability of a developmental psychologist:

> Look and think of the implications of the child, born wanting in mind and perception. If it were born otherwise, it would fail to take in the world around it. It would be completely lost on seeing what it had not known nor seen before. It would be annoyed at seeing itself carried around, wrapped in clothing and diapers, and laid in the cradle, though it cannot do without all that owing to the frailty of its body. Similarly, it

would not be met with the tenderness and love which a child usually enjoys, whenever it insists on having its own way and choice. This shows that to have a mind and a perception that grow gradually is for the child's own good. Do you not see how God has made everything in His creation with the utmost wisdom and perfection?[11]

These are some examples of the profound contemplation of early scholars and worshippers which show their ability to delve into great depths to discover the laws of the Almighty in His creation. This search for cosmic laws is shared by both the contemplative worshipper and the modern scientist, despite the difference in objective and religious conviction. Indeed, the laws and principles which govern the universe are sought by modern experimental scientists to help them predict the cosmic events with great precision. Accurate prediction is also the most important evidence used in the Qur'an to establish the truth of all truths: that this universe has a Creator and a God Who holds it together by the laws that He decreed. Consequently, the Qur'an should be viewed as an invigorating inspiration that appeals to the innate nature entrusted by God in the hearts of human beings to search for these laws that regulate the universe. This is confirmed in the Qur'an:

> It is God Who causes the seed and the date-stone to split and sprout. He causes the living to issue from the dead, and He causes the dead to issue from the living. That is God. How then are you diverted from the truth? He is the One Who cleaves the daybreak. He makes the night for rest and tranquillity, and the sun and the moon for the reckoning [of time]. Such is the judgment and ordering of the Exalted in Power, the Omniscient. (6:95–96)

> And the sun runs its course for a period determined for it; that is the decree of the Exalted in Might, the All-Knowing. And the moon We have assigned phases to it, till it becomes like the old stump of a palm-tree. The sun is not permitted to catch up with the moon, nor can the night outstrip the day. Each swims along in [its own] orbit. (36:38–40)

These two phenomena that demonstrate the accuracy of cosmic

laws and their possible prediction are the main bases of the modern scientific method, without which no experimental science can develop. It is true that the Newtonian clockwork image of the universe has been shaken by the science of relativity and quantum physics; however, this scientific revolution does not imply necessarily that there is no order in the universe, or that if there is one, humankind is not capable of knowing it.

Both Muslim and non-Muslim researchers will receive the same material reward and renown, and both will find pleasure and exciting fulfilment in overcoming the problems of their research. However, when Muslim researchers are truly sincere in their work, their incentives for research and the consequent reward will be much more meaningful than those of their non-Muslim colleagues. Indeed, when they discover the intricate relations within the material, biological and psychosocial phenomena, and observe the work of God and His laws in them, they are actually performing the highest form of worship. To them apply the words of the Qur'an: "Those who truly fear God, among His servants, are those who are knowledgeable" (35:28). If such students sincerely direct their research to the service of God, all their efforts of observation, meditation and contemplation (performed in the laboratory or in the field) will be greatly rewarded. Unfortunately, Muslim students do not seem to understand this sacred message, nor do they realize that they will not be able to achieve much without perseverance. If Muslim researchers viewed their task of observation and contemplation as a form of worship for which they can secure the pleasure of God, then they would be more motivated.

If a believer discovers or invents something which is useful to humanity, it will be considered by God as a constant charity; he will be rewarded for it both in this life and in the hereafter – as his work will continue to benefit all those who use it. Any research performed by a Muslim is also an adherence to the Prophet's directive: "The search for knowledge is the duty of every Muslim."[12]

The positive relationship between refined constant contemplation (as an advanced form of worship) and the progress of scientific knowledge is confirmed by the history of progress in the experimental sciences in the Muslim world. Indeed, there is no doubt that the discoveries and inventions made by Muslim scientists in every field taught Europe the scientific method which forms the basis of modern civilization. Similarly, there is no doubt, at least in the Muslim world, that such progress was a direct result of the Muslim scientists' deep belief in God and their observance of the teachings of their religion to contemplate the heavens and the earth. Their great discoveries and inventions were made because they were diligently searching for the signs of God's wisdom in His creation and the general laws by which He directs the universe.

In her admirable book, *The Sun of Allah Shines on the West*, the German orientalist Sigrid Hunke says:

> Prophet Muhammad urged his followers to contemplate and study the wonders of creation as a means of appreciating the power of the Creator. He also assured his disciples that knowledge enlightens their path of faith. He advised every Muslim man and woman to seek knowledge, making that a religious duty. Seeking knowledge and disseminating it, he preached, is rewarded by God in the same way He rewards worshipping. The reward of learning is like that of fasting, and the reward of teaching is like that of salah or daily prayers.[13]

Hunke affirms that Francis Bacon, Galileo, and other Western scholars were not the ones who established the bases of the scientific method, as claimed by Western historians, but that the real forerunners and teachers of the world in this field were the Muslims. She also proves that Ibn al-Haytham was the real founder of modern physics, and that he was able to reach this position by virtue of his theoretical meditation and close observation. Indeed, while the civilized world of his time could not find an alternative to the theories of Euclid and Ptolemy, which said that the human eye emits beams of light in order to see things, Ibn al-Haytham adamantly disproved this theory. He said: "There are no beams of light emitted from the eye to effect vision. It is the visible objects which reflect the beams to the eye, effecting the vision through the lenses of the eyes."[14] Hunke adds:

> Ibn al-Haytham achieved great success in his study of optics, and surpassed all that was known in that branch of science, thus founding a

> new scientific discipline...He was the first to make experiments, culminating in his invention of the pinhole camera which was the prototype of modern cameras. Thus he proved that the light-beams travel in straight lines...He also studied the difference in density between air and water, and found an explanation for the refraction of light as it goes through transparent media of different densities. From this he was able to calculate the depth of the air-layer surrounding the earth and found it to be 15 km. Thus, he came up with a result unprecedented in precision and correctness...He also discovered the law which governs the impact of light-reflectors and invented the first type of reading spectacles...The influence of this Arab genius on the West was great. His theories have dominated physics, optics and other European sciences until the present day.[15]

She then goes on to enumerate the contribution of other Muslim scholars in astronomy, mathematics, medicine, chemistry, geometry and other fields. She wrote with enthusiasm about Ibn Sīnā (Avicenna) and his book *Al-Qānūn* (Canon of Medicine):

> What great genius is this which embraced all these theoretical and practical aspects of medicine in all its branches, organizing them in such a unique manner, and presenting them in such an original and expressive style that made the book a unique and important achievement among books on medicine of all ages...For many centuries, that book had the greatest influence on the East and the West alike, and in a manner unprecedented in the history of medicine.[16]

Another unbiased orientalist who wrote about the contributions of early Muslim scholars to science during the Middle Ages, is Montgomery Watt. In his book, *The Influence of Islam on Medieval Europe*, he made the following comments on Ibn Sīnā's *Al-Qānūn*:

> [It] is rightly acclaimed as "the culmination and masterpiece of Arabic systematization" (Meyerhof). It was translated into Latin in the twelfth century, and continued to dominate the teaching of medicine in Europe until the end of the sixteenth century at least. There were sixteen

editions of it in the fifteenth century, one being in Hebrew, twenty editions in the sixteenth century and several more in the seventeenth.[17]

Al-Balkhī has already been mentioned in connection with his contributions in cognitive psychology, his delineation of the influence of thought in initiating psychological disorders, and the use of contemplation in their treatment. He was also a Muslim scientist and thinker who offered unequaled contributions to psychiatry. Indeed, he was the first physician to differentiate between neurosis and psychosis, and to classify emotional disorders in a strikingly modern way. He combined deep thinking and contemplation with Islamic teachings to classify neuroses into four types: fear and anxiety (*al-khawf wa al-faza*ᶜ); anger and aggression (*al-ghaḍab*); sadness and depression (*al-ḥuzn wa al-jaza*ᶜ); and obsessions (*al-waswasah*). He clearly attributed the development of emotional disorders to the interaction (*ishtibāk*) between the patient's biological constitution, his environment and his inner cognitive activities. In discussing these psychosomatic aspects and individual differences, al-Balkhī said that since man is composed of a body and a soul, both may show health or sickness, balance or unbalance.[18] Disorders of the body include fever, headache and other physical illnesses; and disorders of the soul include symptoms such as anger, anxiety and sadness.

The titles of the eight chapters on the sustenance of the soul or psyche resemble the contents page of a modern book on psychotherapy and mental hygiene. Indeed, al-Balkhī – who was a master of Arabic prose – clearly differentiates between normal and common, and between extreme emotional reactions of ordinary people and those whose emotional nature has already become pathological. His approach is both preventive and therapeutic and includes a cognitive and psychophysiological approach. In the first two chapters, he stresses the importance of psychological health and how its disorder can be more serious than physical illnesses. The rest of the manuscript details how to overcome anxiety, depression, anger and obsessional neurosis by creative psychospiritual cognitive therapy aided by entertaining concrete illustrations.

For example, when discussing the neuroses associated with fear and anxiety, he gives a number of vivid clinical illustrations of anxiety related to the apprehension of future problems such as losing one's job or one's health, or fear resulting from a phobia of thunder or death. Then, just like modern rational behavior therapists, he states that most of the things that people fear are not rational. To prove his point, he likens the fearful panic-stricken neurotic to a Bedouin who travels to a cold, damp country and sees fog for the first time, and thinks that it is a solid impenetrable object. However, once he enters it, he discovers that it is only damp air, no different from the air he has just been breathing.[19]

Apart from his well-developed therapy for neurotics, al-Balkhī also repeatedly refers to the emotional abnormalities of normal people, describing them as a diminished form of true emotional illness. He does not speak of the so-called neurotic as a 'patient', but rather as a person whose emotional overreactions have become a habit. This, as I have mentioned in an article about al-Balkhī,[20] is a much-needed approach in modern psychiatry and psychotherapy which, by erroneously adopting a medical model, have largely limited themselves to a therapy aimed at the 'sick' instead of one aimed at the psychological healing of 'unhappy souls'.

More importantly, from his contemplation and detailed clinical observation, he was able to classify depression into the three types mentioned in the most recent classification of psychiatric symptoms, DSM-III-R. The first type, which is referred to in the modern classification as 'normal depression', is described by al-Balkhī as the normal everyday sadness that afflicts everybody since "this world is a place which cannot be inhabited without problems and deprivation." However, what is most remarkable is that he was able to differentiate between the second and third kinds of depression – namely, between endogenous depressive disorders originating within the body as a result of internal chemical causes, and those due to exogenous or environmental factors outside the body. In the following quotation that shows his sophisticated clinical insight into these two kinds of depression, readers with psychiatric or clinical psychological knowledge will be able to appreciate the accuracy of his ability to differentiate between them.

> Sadness or depression (*ḥuzn*) is of two kinds. One kind is clearly known to have (environmental) causes, such as the loss of a loved relative, bankruptcy, or the loss of something the depressed person values greatly. The other type has no known cause. It is a sudden affliction of sorrow and distress (*ghummah*) that persists all the time, preventing the afflicted person from physical activity, or from showing any happiness, or enjoying any of the pleasures (*shahawāt*). The patient does not know any clear causes for his lack of activity and distress. This latter type depression which has no known cause in fact has its roots in physical symptoms such as impurity of the blood...and other changes in it. Its treatment is a physical medical one which aims at purifying the blood.[21]

These observations were left unnoticed for nearly eleven centuries only to be inappropriately attributed to Emil Kraepelin, whose work was published toward the end of the nineteenth century and who has consequently been credited for having established our modern system of psychiatric classification.

These, then, are some examples of the development of experimental science in the Muslim world, in an age when the contemplation of God's creation and the laws by which He sustains the universe formed the basis of that scientific renaissance. It was a mature, balanced civilization in which the physical and the spiritual interacted in a harmonious and homogeneous way, based on the realization of the innate dual nature of the human being as a rational animal and a spiritual being. Regrettably, modern Muslim societies have failed to uphold these values that brought supremacy to their forefathers, while Europe has built an advanced technological secular civilization, rooted in a materialistic non-religious worldview.

However, even if Western civilization has succeeded in bringing prosperity and mastery to its people, it has deprived them of satisfying their innate spiritual craving. Indeed, unlike the Islamic civilization, it dismisses the soul and has replaced religion with a new god of secular science. This denial of the soul is in fact the main reason behind the widespread unhappiness and the huge increase of cases of neuroses, psychoses, addiction, crime, suicide, divorce, abortion and the neglect of the elderly in modern Western societies. The stark statistics of such Western social problems show clearly that Muslim societies, in spite of all their shortcomings, enjoy a much happier and more tranquil existence.

If a person's worldview does not include belief in the soul or in the hereafter, it is only natural for him (or her) to be a hedonistic animal trying to enjoy his material life and avoid any painful experiences as much as possible. But when this craving is hampered by life's problems or mere sickness and old age, such individuals will inevitably feel dejected, anxious or depressed, succumb to neurotic and psychotic reactions, or try to deny their deprivation through alcohol, drugs, or suicide. Consequently, if human beings are not believed to have been bestowed with a God-given soul, why should women be expected to bear babies of unwanted pregnancies. Similarly, if people suffer from painful or seemingly incurable diseases and do not believe in a hereafter or the everlasting life of the soul, why should they have to continue this 'senseless' suffering?

The alienation of Islam and the spiritual roots of its civilization is most unfortunate, for it has resulted in the tragic split between the physical and the spiritual, and between science and religion. Never was there such a balanced civilization as the one which prospered under the guidance of Islam, when human knowledge and religion presented themselves in an unprecedented harmony under the aegis of submission to the One Almighty God. Scientists such as Ibn Sīnā, al-Balkhī and Ibn al-Haytham entered their laboratories or hospitals, assured that they were no less esteemed or rewarded by God than worshippers who entered mosques for periods of extended meditation; in fact they earned even more reward and respect.

This may bring to mind the two Qur'anic verses (35:27 and 28) quoted earlier that mention those who acquire knowledge from deep contemplation and remembrance of the greatness of God's creation of peoples and animals of different colors and shapes. There are also a number of hadiths that strongly praise the knowledgeable person over the mere worshipper. In one of these sayings, the Prophet states that the ʿalim, or the one whose deep knowledge leads him to a better appreciation of his Creator, is, in comparison with the worshipper, like the

Prophet in comparison with the weakest in faith among his Companions.[22] This is supported by the ancient Islamic saying: "The ink that flows from the pens of the pious Muslim scholars is better than the blood that flows from the wounds of those who are bloodstained in an Islamic holy war." This exposition also enables a fuller appreciation of the sayings of al-Ḥasan al-Baṣrī and ʿUmar ibn ʿAbd al-ʿAzīz already quoted, that "one hour of contemplation is better than a whole night's vigil in worship," and that "remembrance of God is a good deed, but contemplation of God's favors is the best kind of worship."

We can thus see the contrast between the healthy combination of science and religious belief among early Muslim scholars, and the present situation in the Western world and much of the international scientific community. Sadly, many 'secularized' Muslim scholars have also chosen to follow and adopt the Western model. Nevertheless, and ironically, at the time when Muslims are shying away from the bold Islamization of their human, social and scientific disciplines, the Western world is beginning to recognize the social defacement caused by the schism between science, religion and secularization. Many of their thinkers speak openly against this unnatural split. For instance, in his bestseller, *People of the Lie*, the renowned American psychiatrist Scott Peck states that the main reason for the psychological and psychiatric problems he discusses in his book is this rift:

> The major reason for this strange state of affairs is that the scientific and religious models have hitherto been considered totally immiscible – like oil and water, mutually incompatible and rejecting.
>
> In the late seventeenth century, after the Galileo affair proved hurtful to both, science and religion worked out an unwritten social contract of nonrelationship. The world was quite arbitrarily divided into the 'natural' and the 'supernatural'. Religion agreed that the 'natural world' was the sole province of the scientists. And science agreed, in turn, to keep its nose out of the spiritual – or for that matter, anything to do with values. Indeed, science defined itself as 'value free'.[23]

In one of his more recent books, appropriately titled *Denial of the Soul*, Scott Peck exposes the reasons for the rejection of the 'soul' in

Western science. He strongly attacks this atheistic position as well as the predicament of the religious American professionals who do nothing about it:

> The word 'soul' is probably in the vocabulary of every second-grader...Then why is it that (it) is not in the professional lexicon of psychiatrists, other mental health workers, students of the mind, and physicians in general?
>
> There are two reasons. One is that the concept of God is inherent in the concept of soul, and 'God talk' is virtually off-limits within these relatively secular professions. Religious though individuals in these professions might be personally, they would not want to offend their secular colleagues. Nor, for that matter, would they care to lose their jobs. The fact is that to speak of God or the soul in their professional gatherings would be politically incorrect.
>
> The other reason is that these professionals properly have a taste for intellectual rigor, and the soul is something that cannot be completely defined...It is not the secularists who worry me in relation to the widespread denial of the soul...It is the religious majority who do not take their religion seriously.[24]

In *Timeless Healing*, Benson also blames vehemently "the modern world's replacement of faith with science." He even goes so far as to attribute a genetic aspect to belief in God in order to explain why atheists who go against their genetic code of belief lead a miserable and unfulfilled life. He also explains this hereditary link in terms of the Darwinian evolution, which ironically carries most of the responsibility for the antireligious attitude among Western scientists! This is significant as it approaches the Islamic belief that faith in God is an integral part of human nature (*fiṭrah*), although Islam goes further stating that it originates from the spirit (*rūḥ*) that God breathed into Adam, and is not merely a biological coincidence. Benson writes:

> Even when we (as scientists) acquire new information, even when we conquer mysteries, we feel empty and unfulfilled. And faith is the only long-term solace. In part that is because faith in an Infinite Absolute is

the only adequate counterforce to the ultimate facts of disease and death.

That is why I argue that our genetic blueprint has made believing in an Infinite Absolute (God) part of our nature. By the process of natural selection, mutating genes deemed faith important enough to the survival of our forefathers and mothers that we were endowed with the same tendencies. Ironically then, it can be argued that evolution favors religion, causing our brains to generate the impulses we need to carry on – faith, hope, and love becoming part of the neuromatrix with which we approach living.[25]

It is with great interest that one notices that recent discoveries in secular Western science, which originally came to demote and replace religion, are, in turn, causing a new scientific revolution and a return to this earlier position. Ironically, this process is spearheaded by physics, the 'king' of the exact sciences. No physicist can tell us in better words about this new paradigm than Fritjof Capra, who writes in his Foreword to Ronald Valle and Rolf von Eckartsberg's *Metaphors of Consciousness*:

> Physics has played a major role in shaping the old [Newtonian] paradigm...it has been the shining example of an 'exact' science, and has served as a model for all other sciences. The paradigm that is now shifting comprises...values that have dominated our society for several hundred years...They include belief in the scientific method as the only valid approach to knowledge, and the split between mind and matter, [and] the view of nature as a mechanical system.
>
> In the twentieth century, however, physics went through several conceptual revolutions that clearly revealed the limitations of the mechanistic world-view and that led to an organic, ecological view of the world, showing great similarities to the views of mystics of all ages and traditions.
>
> In modern physics, the question of consciousness has risen in quantum theory with the problem of observation and measurement. The recognition that human consciousness determines, to a large extent, the properties of the observed atomic phenomena has forced physicists to

accept the fact that the sharp Cartesian division between mind and matter, between the observer and the observed, cannot be maintained.[26]

An optimist might hope that such inspiring words would change the hearts of secular and overconfident Western scientists, who still think that they are detached observers of social and physical phenomena and that God has nothing to do with their empirically produced results. Unfortunately, only very few scientists, having deeply penetrated the outer layers of their specialization to arrive at its very core, are beginning to question their previous arrogant position of subduing nature. Benson expresses this idea succinctly: "Polls tell us that the majority of [Western] scientists call themselves atheists. But there is an old saying: 'If a little science takes one away from God, a great deal of science brings one back to God.'"[27]

It is obvious from the writings of Western thinkers such as Scott Peck, Benson and Capra that an appropriate reform which will bring happiness to humanity cannot be achieved fully unless scientific progress is based on a balance between human endeavor and divine guidance. Indeed, this is the only way that scientists will return to and rediscover the love for, commitment to and unity with all of God's creation. In this respect, the Qur'an declares: "And He [the Almighty] has subjected to you all that is in the heavens and on earth. Behold, in that are signs for those who reflect" (45:13).

However, the materialistic secular worldview has sadly inverted this warm attachment between humankind and nature to become a perpetual war and struggle. Every discovery or invention is sensationally announced in the media as a "defeat of nature" as though nature is a constant enemy. Discussing this very issue, Sayyid Quṭb writes:

> The Westerners, the heirs of the misguided Romans, always use the phrase "defeat of nature" instead of "utilizing the forces of nature." This expression is indicative of the misguided secular view, which is estranged from God's divine guidance. But the true Muslim, whose heart is close to his Merciful and Compassionate Lord, whose soul is close to the soul of all creation which glorifies God, the Lord of the universe, is a person who believes that God is the Creator of all these forces,

> and he does not need to fight them, or be their opponent. God created all these forces in accordance with one and the same law, so they can cooperate to fulfil the goals for which they are destined. He subjected them to man from the start and made it possible for man to discover their secrets and laws. Man should thank God whenever he is given a chance to get help from one of these forces. God is the One Who subjects these forces to man; it is not man who conquers and defeats these forces.[28]

The modern world urgently needs to terminate this war by reuniting science and nature in eternal harmony. Then, once that long overdue reconciliation is realized, genuine scientists and scholars will no longer harbor any enmity against the universe nor any desire to conquer nature. They will be like Ibn al-Haytham, Jābir ibn Ḥayyān and al-Khwarazmī, who attained their great scientific achievements by contemplating God's creation with open hearts and discerning minds.

In their close relationship with all the elements of God's creation, Muslim scientists of the past were in fact influenced by the example and sayings of the Prophet. Indeed, he often spoke about inanimate objects in nature with the feeling of sharing with them submission to the Almighty God. Once, for instance, during his Hijrah to Madinah, he addressed the new moon with intimate affection combined with love and reverence for God Who created both the moon and himself and to Whom both were echoing His praise. He said: "O crescent of good and guidance, my faith is in Him who created you. [O crescent] Our Lord and yours is God."[29] The Prophet also addressed Mount Uhud in Madinah in the most affectionate words and said to his Companions: "Uhud is a mountain that loves us and we love it."[30]

If such love and affection can be directed towards inanimate things in nature, the reader can imagine the genuine love that the Prophet had for plants, animals and other human beings. It is reported that the Prophet said that a woman would be thrown into hell for having locked up her cat until it died of thirst and hunger.[31] On the other hand, a prostitute would be admitted to paradise because she climbed down a well to collect water for a thirsty dog in the desert.[32] It is thus very difficult for Muslims to regard nature as an enemy to be conquered rather than a friend to be appreciated.

CHAPTER NINE

Conclusion

In this study, I have tried to delineate the significance of *tafakkur* or meditative contemplation of God's creation as a religious duty for all Muslims, and show that the Qur'an and the hadiths of Prophet Muhammad abound with teachings that urge Muslims to regularly worship God by reflecting on His creation. These teachings use all kinds of methods, such as praising the worshippers who are engaged in this blessed activity and condemning the unbelievers who do not reflect on their own creation or the creation of the world in which they live. In fact, no Muslim can offer salah or perform dhikr (remembrance of God) without engaging in some form of contemplation of His bounties and unlimited Omnipotence; similarly, contemplation cannot be accomplished without remembrance. As I have explained, they are like two sides of the same coin.

Furthermore, if Muslims wish to ascend the spiritual path of devoted worshippers in their transcendental journey to the stage of spiritual enlightenment and insightful cognition (*shuhūd*), they will find no substitute for deep meditative contemplation. Indeed, as they gradually refine their contemplative endowment from mere sense perception to actual insightful cognition, they will reach the blessed stage in which their heart and mind become overwhelmed with the love and glorification of the Almighty, and will see with both their physical sight and spiritual insight that everything in this universe totally submits to God, subservient to His will and tendered by His mercy and compassion. As many Muslim scholars and sages have testified, worshippers who attain this level are the happiest of people. They secure the pleasure of God as well as tranquillity, blissfulness and beatitude in this world.

The Muslim reader who wishes to climb this spiritual ladder will,

I hope, have benefited from the discussion on the individual differences between Muslim contemplators in attaining a high degree of cognitive insight and the nine factors that influence the depth of this blessed activity. The aspiring reader should then explore his spiritual endowments, his inherited ability to concentrate and his positive environmental conditions. He should also try to look for the bad habits and other disturbing aspects that deter him from contemplation in order to get rid of them and neutralize them with counter factors. If he sincerely and diligently seeks to do this, the sphere of his contemplation will expand until it is deeply and habitually inculcated in his psychological and spiritual system.

However, people vary in their endeavor to improve their ability to contemplate as well as in the practices that are more suitable for them. For instance, whereas some people may benefit from emulating the deep contemplative behavior of a blessed model, others may be moved by increasing their knowledge about the fine intricacies of God's universe in tiny creatures and distant galaxies, or may find prayers and remembrance of God performed at night and during the early hours of the morning more effective. There is no doubt that a person who is sincere and highly motivated will be guided to a better knowledge of God and to spiritual enlightenment. It must be stressed, however, that any permanent change in behavior cannot be attained without the devotion of time and energy – and spiritual improvement is no exception.

I hope that the two first chapters of this book on contemplation from a psychological perspective and the contributions of early Muslim scholars will be an eye-opener for my colleagues in the fields of psychology and psychotherapy, particularly those who are still emulating Western models. Indeed, if European psychologists are complaining about the Americanization of psychology in spite of all their cultural similarities, how can we, as Muslims and Third World professionals be expected to continue resorting to their theories and practices, including those that have not even been used in their own Western societies? In fact, Western psychologists have now come to realize that this exportation of inappropriate Americanized psychology to Third World countries is a practice that can only perpetuate dependency and exploitative traditions reminiscent of colonialism. In an article entitled 'But is it a science? Traditional and alternative approaches to social behavior', two psychologists, F. Moghaddam from Georgetown University and R. Harre from Oxford University, very lucidly explored the pitfalls of mental slavery to 'Americanized' Western psychology in Third World countries:

> ...the most important factor shaping psychology in the international context continues to be power inequalities between and within nations. The inability of psychology to contribute to Third World development arises in large part from these inequalities...and surely *this is an unethical issue*. Putative psychological 'knowledge' which is of highly questionable reliability and validity even in the Western context is being exported wholesale to Third World societies, as part of a large exchange system ultimately driven by profits. [my italics]

They continue by highlighting the current hegemony of American psychology over the rest of the world and how this can foster submission and dependency among students of psychology in developing countries:

> The United States has established itself as the only psychology Superpower...Psychology continues to be exported from the U.S. to the rest of the world, with little or no serious attention given to the appropriateness of what is being exported...Similarly, Third World psychologists are trained in the U.S. and in other Western countries, without regard to the question of the appropriateness of their training. Indeed, the continued exportation...and inappropriate trained personnel from Western to Third World societies *strengthens ties of dependency and continues exploitative traditions established through colonialism*. [my italics][1]

Western psychology in general and psychotherapy in particular have for many years been led astray by secular theories and practices that were finally discredited as inappropriate, useless or at times outright harmful. For example, Freud's psychoanalytic theories and therapy with its misleading emphasis on unconscious sexual and aggressive motivation has ruled over Western psychotherapy for more than 70 years only to be replaced by a radical behavioristic paradigm. Though more successful with minor and specific disorders such as phobias, behavior therapy is no less hostile than psychoanalysis to the spiritual aspects in human nature. However, with the advent of the contemporary cognitive revolution, Western psychotherapists are finally beginning to recognize the great influence of consciousness and mind in their patients, which would eventually lead them to respect their religious and spiritual beliefs.

This is a real revolution in that it is now realized that it is neither the unconscious sexual conflict nor the environmental stimuli per se which cause emotional disorders, but rather the perceptions, thoughts and contemplation of the person about these stimuli or experiences which can make him a neurotic. Thus, after many years of wandering in the desert of soulless theories, psychotherapy is finally returning to the common-sense practices of cognitive healing that has always been used to help the emotionally disturbed. As I mentioned in the chapter on the works of early Muslim scholars on Islamic cognitive psychology, these cognitive therapeutic methods were meticulously studied and described by our ancient Muslim physicians and healers.

Thus, if a person is religiously oriented, all his conceptions and understanding about what he experiences in this world would be colored by these beliefs. Helping him psychologically without probing and making use of his spiritual orientations is bound to fail. Accordingly, if a therapist clings to an outmoded Western model of a secular non-judgmental approach, he is bound to fail with Muslim clients whose worldview is moulded by Islam as a religion and a way of life.

As for Muslim scientists, and particularly those who spend most of their time in research and laboratory investigations, I hope that they will find the chapter on the Muslim scientist as a contemplating worshipper pertinent. Indeed, many young science students think that scientists strictly follow the steps of empirical, inductive and deductive methods when striving to invent new technologies or discover new phenomena. However, these clearly defined steps for identifying a problem, formulating a hypothesis, experimenting and collecting data and testing the hypothesis – which are thoroughly studied by all undergraduate science students – are simply broad guidelines. In fact, deep thinking and contemplation which result in unexpected intuition are much more common than scientists would be willing to confess. At times, a discovery or invention may even be the result of a 'mistake' that happened by chance to occur and be recorded in a laboratory.

The spiritually motivated Muslim scientist who strongly believes that what he is looking for is 'out there' in God's boundless knowledge, and that through hard work, deep contemplation and prayer he will be enlightened with a solution to his problem, is definitely more of a worshipper than someone who is merely praying in a mosque. Indeed, we often forget the value of prayer (salah) and invocation (*duʿā*) in solving our intellectual problems and relieving our distress, though God says in the Qur'an that He is the One Who listens to the distressed soul when it calls on Him, and Who relieves its suffering (27:62).

The suffering of a scientist patiently waiting for a new insight can only be appreciated by those who have experienced similar distress. I have personally known two devoted Muslim students who were studying for their M.Sc. and Ph.D. and were facing great difficulties in finding any useful results. They would spend long hours in their laboratories working alone and praying to God for a solution. One of them, at the American University of Beirut, used to assemble his apparatus, start the experiment going, then prostrate himself in a very long *sujūd* pleading God for a breakthrough, prostrating with his forehead on the bare floor of the lab. Then they were suddenly bestowed with the correct chemical procedures – one of them as an intuition, and the other by a vivid dream in which he received a chemical formula and was told to record it as soon as he woke up from his sleep.

Modern secular psychologists and some westernized Muslims may explain such phenomena in terms of Gestalt insightful learning (in which monkeys suddenly get the idea of fixing two short sticks together in order to get a banana that is out of reach of either stick) or in terms of latent learning. Dreams are viewed as wish fulfilment of unconscious sexual and aggressive impulses, as a way used by the brain to erase unwanted information – i.e. the exact opposite to what happened to the afore-mentioned Muslim chemists – or simply as meaningless random nerve firings to which the brain tries to give meaning. The spiritual dimension of dreams as carriers of divine knowledge does not exist in such a secular worldview.

Western scientists hold on to such materialistic explanations because they do not want to transcend the physical; God, or even the 'spiritual', are not recognized as possible means to explain a phenomenon. Instead, they assume that by describing the event in secular terms and inventing a new term for its 'functioning', they have already solved its mystery, and when the term is used, the psychologist has the false impression of certainty. At times such terms are even used in a circular fashion to 'explain' other psychological events. For example, the vague term 'suggestion' is often explained as what happens during hypnosis, and 'hypnosis' is defined as an altered state of consciousness in which suggestion plays a major role. The real nature of hypnosis and suggestion are still very ambiguous in modern psychology, perhaps because they do not lend themselves to a simple behavioristic paradigm.

As Muslim professionals we should be careful in following such a secular trend. Even if a psychological event or theory has been repeatedly confirmed by empirical evidence, we need to remind ourselves about the One Who created this psychological reality and look for the divine wisdom for such a principle. In accepting any learning theory or practice, we should always attribute it to the principles and ways that God has chosen to bestow us with knowledge and be thankful to Him, since no human will gain any form of knowledge without His permission as He states in the Qur'an.

NOTES

INTRODUCTION

1 Hadith reported by Abū Saʿīd al-Ḥākim in Jalāl al-Dīn al-Suyūṭī, *Al-Jāmiʿ al-Ṣaghīr*, vol. 1 (Beirut: Dār al-Fikr, 1981), p.273.

2 Cited in Imām Zayn al-Dīn Aḥmad ibn ʿAbd al-Laṭīf al-Zubaydī, *Mukhtaṣṣ Ṣaḥīḥ al-Bukhārī*, vol. 1 (Beirut: Dār al-Kutub al-ʿIlmiyyah, 1993), p.31, Hadith no.47.

3 To "stand before God" means to sincerely seek the truth; "in pairs or alone" means free from the influence and pressure of the collective mind.

AUTHOR'S INTRODUCTION

1 (ṢAAS) – *Ṣallā Allāhu ʿalayhi wa sallam*. May the peace and blessings of God be upon him. Said whenever the name of Prophet Muhammad is mentioned.

CHAPTER ONE

1 J. B. Watson, *Behaviourism* (London: W. Norton & Co., 1970), p.ix.

2 Ibid.

3 John Eccles, *Evolution of the Brain: Creation of the Self* (London: Routledge Publishers, 1991), p.225.

4 Malik B. Badri, *ʿIlm al-Nafs min Manẓūr Islāmī*, (Khartoum: IIIT, 1987).

5 In H. J. Eysenck, *Psychology is about People* (London: The Penguin Press, 1972), p.300.

6 Thomas Kuhn, *The Structure of Scientific Revolutions* (Chicago: University of Chicago Press, 1970).

7 Eccles, *Evolution of the Brain*.

8 Ibid.

9 Karl Popper and John Eccles, *The Self and Its Brain* (London: Routledge Publishers, 1990), p.372.

10 W. Uttal, *The Psychobiology of the Mind* (London: John Wiley Publishers, 1978).

11 J. C. Pearce, *Evolution's End* (San Francisco: Harper Collins Publishers, 1992), pp. 103 and 104.

12 Cited in ibid., p.103.

13 Ibid., p.104.

14 Ibid., pp.104 and 105.

15 Abū Ḥāmid al-Ghazālī, *Iḥyāʾ ʿUlūm al-Dīn* (Beirut: Dār al-Qalam, n.d.).

16 Yūsuf Bashīr al-Tijānī, *Dīwān Ishrāqah* (Beirut: Dār al-Thaqāfah, 1972).

17 Abbās Maḥmūd al-ʿAqqād, *Al-Lughah al-Shāʿirah* (Cairo: Maktabat Gharīb, n.d.).

18 Ibid, p.70.

19 Anwar al-Jundī, *Al-Fuṣḥā: Lughat al-Qur'ān* (Beirut: Dār al-Kitāb al-Lubnānī, 1982), p.27.

CHAPTER TWO

1 Ibn Qayyim al-Jawziyyah, *Miftāḥ Dār al-Saʿādah* (Riyadh: Ri'āsat al-Iftā', n.d.), p.183.

2 Abū Zayd al-Balkhī, *Maṣāliḥ al-Abdān wa al-Anfus*, MS 3741 (Istanbul: Ayasofya Library). Photocopied by the Institute of Arabic-Islamic Sciences, Frankfurt A.M., 1984.

3 Aaron T. Beck, *Cognitive Therapy and the Emotional Disorders* (New York: New American Library, 1976), pp.29–35.

4 Ibn Qayyim al-Jawziyyah, *Al-Fawā'id* (Beirut: Dār al-Nafā'is, 1981), p.173.

5 Ibid.

6 Al-Ghazālī, *Iḥyā'*, vol. 3, pp.56–59.

7 Ibid.

8 Ibid.

9 Abū Ḥāmid al-Ghazālī, *Al-Ḥikmah fī Makhlūqāt Allāh* (Beirut: Dār Iḥyā' al-ʿUlūm, 1984), pp.13 and 14.

10 Ibn al-Qayyim, *Miftāḥ*, p.180.

11 Ibid.

12 Al-Ghazālī, *Iḥyā'*, vol. 4, p.389.

13 Ibid., p.388.

14 Ibid., pp.388–389.

15 Ibn al-Qayyim, *Miftāḥ*, p.180.

16 Ibn Qayyim al-Jawziyyah, *Madārij al-Sālikīn*, ed. ʿAbd al-Munʿim al-Ṣāliḥ (The Emirates: Wizārat al-Awqāf, n.d.).

17 Ibn Taymiyyah, *Majmūʿ Fatāwā al-Imām Aḥmad ibn Taymiyyah*, vol. 10 (Riyadh: Maṭābiʿ al-Riyāḍ, n.d.), pp. 221–225.

18 Muḥammad al-Ghazālī, *Fiqh al-Sīrah* (Beirut: Dār al-Kutub al-Ḥadīthah, 1960), p.190.

19 Ibid.

20 It may be of interest in this connection to mention that during the entire period in which Freud wrote his major sexually laden theories he was addicted to cocaine; thus, much of the sex-related theories that we teach our students as 'science' is, in fact, the incoherent narration of an ingenious drug addict. See E. M. Thornton, *Freud and Cocaine: The Freudian Fallacy* (London: Blond & Briggs Publishers, 1983).

CHAPTER THREE

1 See Malik B. Badri, *The Aids Crisis: An Islamic Socio-Cultural Perspective* (Malaysia: ISTAC Publications, 1997).

2 I. S. Bengelsdorf, 'Alcohol and morphine addictions believed to be chemically similar', 5 March 1970, *Los Angeles Times*, II, 7, cited in R. C. Carson, J. N. Butcher and J. C. Coleman, *Abnormal Psychology and Modern Life*, 8th edn. (London: Scott, Foreman & Co., 1988), p.368.

3 Herbert Benson, *Timeless Healing* (London: Simon & Schuster, 1996), pp.272–274. See also Susan R. Burchfield, *Stress: Psychological and Physiological Interactions* (London: McGraw Hill Books, 1985), p.113.

4 'Organically minded' is a common description for medical practitioners who belittle the psychological aspects in the etiology of disorders and who exaggerate the physiological aspects and the importance of drugs.

5 Herbert Benson, *Beyond the Relaxation Response: How to Harness the Healing Power of your Personal Beliefs* (New York: Berkley Books, 1985).

6 Benson, *Timeless Healing*.

7 S. Wolf, 'Effects of Suggestion and Conditioning on the Action of Chemical Agents on Human Subjects: the Pharmacology of Placebos', *Journal of Clinical Investigation* 29 (1950), pp.100–109.

8 J. P. Pinel, *Biopsychology* (Boston: Allyn & Bacon, 1993), pp.591–593.

9 Benson, *Beyond the Relaxation Response*.

10 Ibid.

11 Ibid.

12 Ibid.

13 L. Le Shan, *How to Meditate* (London: Bantam Books, 1988).

14 Ibid., p.109.

15 Benson, *Beyond the Relaxation Response*, p.111.

16 Abūl Aʿlā Mawdūdī, *Mabādi' al-Islām* (Damascus: Dār al-Qur'ān al-Karīm, 1977).

17 Benson, *Timeless Healing*.

18 Ibid, p.177.

19 See Ahmed Elkadi, 'Quranic Concepts for Eliminating Negative Emotions: Another Aspect of the Healing Effects of the Quran', unpublished paper presented at the 5th International Conference on the Scientific Signs of Quran and Sunnah, Moscow, Russia, September 1993.

20 See Muhammad Khair al-Irgisoosi, 'The Influence of Muscular Relaxation and Islamic Prayer in the Treatment of Essential Hypertension', Ph.D. thesis (University of Khartoum, 1992). The study was originally registered for the M.A. degree, but was elevated to Ph.D. for its thoroughness and contributions, and the degree was conferred in 1992.

21 Benson, *Timeless Healing*, p.158.

22 Cited in ibid., pp.158–159.

23 Le Shan, *How to Meditate*, p.77.

24 Ibn al-Qayyim, *Madārij al-Sālikīn*, pp.31–32.

25 Ibn Taymiyyah, *Majmūʿ Fatāwā*, vol.10, p.647.

CHAPTER FOUR

1 Yūsuf ʿAlī, *The Holy Qur'ān: Text Translation and Commentary* (Maryland: Amana Corporation, 1989), p.582, fn.1788 for verse 12:105.

2 Sayyid Quṭb, *Fī Ẓilāl al-Qur'ān*,

vol. 5 (Beirut: Dār al-Shurūq, n.d.), p.2809.

3 Al-Ḥāfiẓ ibn Kathīr, *Tafsīr al-Qur'ān al-ʿAẓīm*, vol. 1 (Beirut: Dār al-Maʿrifah, 1969), p.438.

4 Benson, *Timeless Healing*, pp.68–69 and 74.

5 Quṭb, *Fī Ẓilāl al-Qur'ān*, vol. 6, pp.3279–3280.

CHAPTER FIVE

1 Translation and commentary on this verse by Muhammad Asad, *The Message of the Qur'ān* (Gibraltar: Dār al-Andalus, 1980): "'And we taught him [David] how to make garments [of God consciousness] for you, so that they might fortify you against all that may cause you fear. But are you grateful [for this boon]?' The noun *labūs*...signifies 'a garment'...But since this term has occasionally been used by pre-Islamic Arabs in the sense of 'mail' or 'coats of mail', the classical commentators assume that it has this meaning in the above text as well...Accordingly, they understand the term *ba's*...in its secondary sense of 'war' or 'warlike violence', and interpret the relevant part of the verse thus: 'We taught him how to make coats of mail for you, so that they may fortify you against [the effect of] your warlike violence'. One should, however, bear in mind that *ba's* signifies also 'harm', 'misfortune', 'distress', etc. as well as 'danger'; hence it denotes, in its widest sense, anything that *causes* distress or fear. If we adopt this last meaning, the term *labūs* may be understood in its primary significance of 'garment' – in this case, the metaphorical 'garment of God-consciousness' (*libās al-taqwā*) of which the Qur'an speaks in 7:26. Rendered in this sense, the above verse expresses the idea that the Almighty taught David how to imbue his followers with that deep God-consciousness which frees men from all spiritual distress and all fears, whether it be fear of one another or the subconscious fear of the Unknown. The concluding rhetorical question, 'but are you grateful [for this boon]?' implies that, as a rule, man does not fully realize – and, hence, is not really grateful for – the spiritual bounty thus offered him by God." See p.497, fn.74 for verse 21:80.

CHAPTER SIX

1 Ibn al-Qayyim, *Al-Fawā'id*, p.235.

2 Al-Suyūṭī, *Al-Jāmiʿ*, vol. 1, p.514.

3 Muḥammad Ibrāhīm al-Fayūmī, *Al-Imām al-Ghazālī wa ʿAlāqāt al-Yaqīn bi al-ʿAql* (Cairo: Dār al-Fikr al-ʿArabī, n.d.), pp.38–39.

4 Ibn al-Qayy[illegible] *Al-Fawā'id*, p.235.

5 Al-Ghaz[illegible] 4, p.62. See also, al-[illegible]*nem-brance* [illegible]*fter Life (Book X*[illegible]*m al-dīn)*. Tra[illegible]oduction by T. J. Winte[illegible]dge: Islamic Texts Socie[illegible]1989).

6 Authenticated by Bukhārī and Muslim and recorded by Abū Zakariyyah al-Nawawī, *Riyadh al-Ṣāliḥīn*, English translation by Madani Abbasi, vol. 2 (Riyadh: Al-Maṭbaᶜah al-Duwaliyyah al-Islāmiyyah, n.d.), p.920.

7 Aḥmad ibn Ḥanbal, *Kitāb al-Zuhd* (Beirut: Dār al-Kutub al-ᶜIlmiyyah, 1983), p. 398.

8 Authenticated by Malik and Tirmidhī and recorded by Muḥammad ibn Sulaymān, *Jamᶜ al-Fawā'id*, vol. 2 (Cyprus: Bank Fayṣal al-Islāmī, 1985).

9 Authenticated by Aḥmad ibn Ḥanbal in *Al-Musnad* (n.d.) and documented by Muḥammad Nāṣir al-Dīn al-Albānī, *Ṣaḥīḥ al-Jamīᶜ al-Ṣaghīr lī al-Suyūṭī wa Ziyādah* (Beirut: Al-Maktab al-Islāmī, 1986), p.931, Hadith no. 5250.

10 Al-Ḥārith al-Muḥāsibī, *Kitāb al-Tawahhum* (Aleppo: Dār al-Waᶜy, n.d.), pp.1–18.

11 Sayyid Quṭb, *In the Shade of the Qur'an*, vol. 30 (London: MWH Publishers, 1979), pp.62–65.

CHAPTER SEVEN

1 Al-Ghazālī, *Iḥyā'*, vol. 4, pp.388–389.

2 H. J. Eysenck, *The Structure of Human Personality* (London: Methuen, 1970).

3 See Badri, *AIDS Crisis*.

4 Authenticated by Bukhārī and recorded in al-Suyūṭī, *Al-Jāmiᶜ*, vol. 1, p.235.

5 Fritjof Capra, *The Tao of Physics* (Glasgow: Harper Collins Publishers, 1992), p.11.

6 Quoted by Abū Ḥurayrah and recorded by al-Tirmidhī.

7 Ibn al-Qayyim, *Madārij*, p. 632.

8 Ibn al-Jawzī, *Ṣaid al-Khāṭir*, ed. ᶜAlī al-Ṭanṭāwī (Damascus: Dār al-Fikr, 1978), pp. 148-149.

CHAPTER EIGHT

1 See L. Malpass, *Human Behavior* (New York: McGraw Hill, 1966), p.3.

2 See John Clover Monsma (ed.), *Evidence of God in an Expanding Universe* (G. P. Putman & Sons Publishers, 1958).

3 Al-Ghazālī, *Al-Ḥikmah*, pp.87–95.

4 Muṣṭafā Maḥmūd, *Lughz al-Ḥayāh* (Cairo: Dār al-Nahḍah al-ᶜArabiyyah, n.d.), pp.47–49.

5 Ali ibn Abu Talib, *Nahjul Balagha: Peak of Eloquence*. Translated by Sayed Ali Reza (New York: Tahrike Tarsile Qur'an, Inc., 1985), pp.370–371.

6 Ibn al-Qayyim, *Miftāḥ*, vol. 1, pp. 242–243.

7 Ibid.

8 Al-Zamakhsharī, *Tafsīr al-Kashshāf* (Cairo: Al-Maktabah al-Tijariyyah, 1354AH), vol.1, p.57.

9 Ibid.

10 Al-Ghazālī, *Al-Ḥikmah*, p.83.

11 Ibid., p.68.

12 Quoted by Anas in al-Suyūtī, *Al-Jāmi*ᶜ, vol.2, p.182.

13 Sigrid Hunke, *The Sun of Allah Shines on the West.* Translated into Arabic by Faruq Baydun and Kamal Dasuqi (Beirut: Dār al-Āfāq al-Jadīdah, n.d.), p. 369.

14 Ibid.

15 Ibid.

16 Ibid., p.289.

17 W. Montgomery Watt, *The Influence of Islam on Medieval Europe* (Edinburgh: Edinburgh University Press, 1987), p.38.

18 Al-Balkhī, *Maṣāliḥ al-Abdān*, pp.270–271.

19 Ibid., p.307.

20 Malik B. Badri, 'Abū Zayd al-Balkhī: A Genius Whose Contributions to Psychiatry Needed more than Ten Centuries to be Appreciated', *Malaysian Journal of Psychiatry*, vol.6, no.2, September 1999, pp.48–53.

21 Al-Balkhī, *Maṣāliḥ*, pp. 316–319.

22 Al-Albānī, *Ṣaḥīḥ al-Jamī*ᶜ *al-Ṣaghīr*, vol. 2, p.776.

23 M. Scott Peck, *People of the Lie: Hope for Healing Human Evil* (London: Arrow Books, 1990), p.43.

24 M. Scott Peck, *Denial of the Soul: Spiritual and Medical Perspectives on Euthanasia and Mortality* (Hemel Hempstead, UK: Simon & Schuster, 1997), pp.129 and 131.

25 Benson, *Timeless Healing*, pp.202 and 208.

26 Ronald S. Valle and Rolf von Eckartsberg, *Metaphors of Consciousness* (New York: Plenum Press, 1981; London: Plenum Publishing, 1994), pp.ix–xii.

27 Ibid., p.200.

28 Quṭb, *Fī Ẓilāl al-Qur'ān*, vol.1, pp.25–26.

29 Authenticated by al-Tirmidhī and recorded in Muḥyi al-Dīn al-Nawawī, *Al-Āthār al-Muntakhabah min Kalām Sayyid al-Abrār* (Beirut: Al-Maktabah al-Thaqāfiyyah, 1983), p.171.

30 Reported by Anas in Bukhārī and Muslim and recorded in al-Suyūṭī, *Al-Jāmi*ᶜ, vol. 1, p.332, Hadith no.2176.

31 Authenticated by Bukhārī and recorded in al-Suyūṭī, *Al-Jāmi*ᶜ, vol. 1, p.646, Hadith no. 4191.

32 Authenticated by Bukhārī and recorded in ibn Sulaymān, *Jam*ᶜ *al-Fawā'id*, vol.2, p.476, Hadith no. 10/8294.

CHAPTER NINE

1 *Journal of World Psychology*, 1:4, 1995, pp.53–54.

BIBLIOGRAPHY

al-Albānī, Muḥammad Nāṣir al-Dīn, *Ṣaḥīḥ al-Jamīʿ al-Ṣaghīr lī al-Suyūṭī wa Ziyādah* (Beirut: Al-Maktab al-Islāmī, 1986).

al-ʿAqqād, ʿAbbās Maḥmūd, *Al-Lughah al-Shāʿirah* (Cairo: Maktabat Gharīb, n.d.).

Ali ibn Abu Talib, *Nahjul Balagha: Peak of Eloquence*. Translated by Sayed Ali Reza (New York: Tahrike Tarsile Qur'an, Inc., 1985).

ʿAlī, Yūsuf, *The Holy Qur'ān: Text Translation and Commentary* (Maryland: Amana Corporation, 1989).

Armstrong, Karen, *A History of God: From Abraham to the Present: A 4,000-Year Quest for God* (London: Heinemann, 1993)

Asad, Muhammad, *The Message of the Qur'ān* (Gibraltar: Dār al-Andalus, 1980).

Badri, Malik B., *ʿIlm al-Nafs min Manẓūr Islāmī* (Khartoum: IIIT Publications, 1987).

——'Abū Zayd al-Balkhī: A Genius Whose Contributions to Psychiatry Needed more than Ten Centuries to be Appreciated', *Malaysian Journal of Psychiatry*, vol.6, no.2, September 1999, pp.48–53.

——*The AIDS Crisis: An Islamic Socio-Cultural Perspective* (Malaysia: ISTAC Publications, 1997).

al-Balkhī, Abū Zayd, *Maṣāliḥ al-Abdān wa al-Anfus*, MS 3741 (Istanbul: Ayasofya Library). Photocopied by the Institute of Arabic-Islamic Sciences, Frankfurt A.M., 1984.

Beck, Aaron T., *Cognitive Therapy and the Emotional Disorders* (New York: New American Library, 1976)

Benson, Herbert, *Beyond the Relaxation Response: How to Harness the Healing Power of your Personal Beliefs* (New York: Berkley Books, 1985).

——*Timeless Healing* (London: Simon & Schuster, 1996).

Capra, Fritjof, *The Tao of Physics* (Glasgow: Harper Collins Publishers, 1992).

Carson, R. C., Butcher, J. N., and Coleman, J. C., *Abnormal Psychology and Modern Life*, 8th edn. (London: Scott, Foresman & Co., 1988).

Eccles, J., *Evolution of the Brain: Creation of the Self* (London: Routledge Publishers, 1991).

Elkadi, Ahmed, 'Quranic Concepts for Eliminating Negative Emotions: Another Aspect of the Healing Effects of the Quran', unpublished paper presented at the 5th International Conference on the Scientific Signs of Quran and Sunnah, Moscow, Russia, September 1993.

Eysenck, H. J., *The Structure of Human Personality* (London: Methuen, 1970).

——*Psychology is about People* (London: The Penguin Press, 1972).

al-Fayūmī, Muḥammad Ibrāhīm, *Al-Imām al Ghazālī wa ʿAlāqāt al-Yaqīn bi al-ʿAql* (Cairo: Dār al-Fikr al-ʿArabī, n.d.).

al-Ghazālī, Abū Ḥāmid, *Al-Ḥikmah fī Makhlūqāt Allāh* (Beirut: Dār Iḥyā' al-ʿUlūm, 1984).

——*Iḥyā' ʿUlūm al-Dīn* (Beirut: Dār al-Qalam, n.d.).

——*The Remembrance of Death and the After Life (Book XL of the Iḥya' ʿulūm al-dīn)*. Translated with introduction by T. J. Winter (Cambridge: Islamic Texts Society, 1989)

al-Ghazālī, Muḥammad, *Fiqh al-Sīrah* (Beirut: Dār al-Kutub al-Hadīthah, 1960).

Ibn Ḥanbal, Aḥmad, *Kitāb al-Zuhd* (Beirut: Dār al-Kutub al-ʿIlmiyyah, 1983).

Ibn al-Jawzī, *Ṣaid al-Khāṭir*, ed. ʿAlī al-Ṭanṭāwī (Damascus: Dār al-Fikr, 1978).

Ibn Kathīr, al-Ḥāfiẓ, *Tafsīr al-Qur'ān al-ʿAẓīm*, vol. 1 (Beirut: Dār al-Maʿrifah, 1969).

Ibn Qayyim al-Jawziyyah, *Al-Fawā'id* (Beirut: Dār al-Nafā'is, 1981).

——*Miftāḥ Dār al-Saʿādah* (Riyadh: Ri'āsat al-Iftā', n.d.).

——*Madārij al-Sālikīn*, ed. ʿAbd al-Munʿim al-Ṣāliḥ (The Emirates: Wizārat al-Awqāf, n.d.).

Ibn Sulayman, Muḥammad, *Jamʿa al-Fawā'id*, vol. 2 (Cyprus: Bank Fayṣal al-Islāmī, 1985).

Ibn Taymiyyah, *Majmūʿ Fatāwā al-Imām Aḥmad ibn Taymiyyah*, vol. 10 (Riyadh: Maṭābiʿ al-Riyād, n.d.).

al-Irgisoosi, Muhammad Khair, 'The Influence of Muscular Relaxation and Islamic Prayer in the Treatment of Essential Hypertension', Ph.D. thesis (University of Khartoum: 1992).

al-Jundī, Anwar, *Al-Fuṣḥā: Lughat al-Qur'ān* (Beirut: Dār al-Kitāb al-Lubnānī, 1982).

Kuhn, Thomas, *The Structure of Scientific Revolutions* (Chicago: University of Chicago Press, 1970).

Le Shan, L, *How to Meditate* (London: Bantam Books, 1988).

Maḥmūd Muṣṭafā, *Lughz al-Ḥayāh* (Cairo: Dār al-Nahḍah al-ʿArabiyyah, n.d.).

Malpass, L., *Human Behavior* (New York: McGraw-Hill, 1966).

Mawdūdī, Abul Aʿlā, *Mabādi' al-Islām* (Damascus: Dār al-Qur'ān al-Karīm, 1977).

Monsma, John Clover (ed.), *Evidence of God in an Expanding Universe* (G. P. Putman & Sons Publishers, 1958)

al-Muḥāsibī, al-Ḥārith, *Kitāb al-Tawahhum* (Aleppo: Dār al-Waʿy, n.d.).

al-Nawawī, Abū Zakariyyah, *Riyadh al-Ṣāliḥīn*, English translation by Madani Abbasi, vol. 2 (Riyadh: Al-Maṭbaʿah al-Duwaliyyah al-Islāmiyyah, n.d.).

al-Nawawī, Muhyi al-Dīn, *Al-Āthār al-Muntakhabah min Kalām Sayyid al-Abrār* (Beirut: Al-Maktabah al-Thaqafiyyah, 1983).

Pearce, J. C., *Evolution's End* (San Francisco: Harper Collins Publishers, 1992).

Peck, M. Scott, *People of the Lie: Hope for Healing Human Evil* (London: Arrow Books, 1990).

——*Denial of the Soul: Spiritual and Medical Perspectives on Euthanasia and Mortality* (Hemel Hemptead, UK: Simon & Schuster, 1997).

Pinel, J. P., *Biopsychology* (Boston: Allyn & Bacon, 1993).

Popper, Karl and Eccles, John, *The Self and Its Brain* (London: Routledge Publishers, 1990).

Quṭb, Sayyid, *Fī Ẓilāl al-Qur'ān*, vol. 5 (Beirut: Dār al-Shurūq, n.d.).

——*In the Shade of the Qur'an*, vol. 30 (London: MWH Publishers, 1979).

al-Suyūṭī, Jalāl al-Dīn, *Al-Jāmiʿ al-Ṣaghīr fī Aḥādīth al-Bashīr al-Nathīr*, vols. 1 and 2 (Beirut: Dār al-Fikr, 1981).

al-Tijānī, Yūsuf Bashīr, *Dīwān Ishrāqah* (Beirut: Dār al-Thaqāfah, 1972).

E.M. Thornton, *Freud and Cocaine: The Freudian Fallacy* (London: Blond & Briggs, 1983).

Uttal, W., *The Psychobiology of the Mind* (London: John Wiley Publishers, 1978).

Valle, Ronald S. and von Eckartsberg, Rolf, *Metaphors of Consciousness* (New York: Plenum Press, 1981; London: Plenum Publishing, 1994).

Watson, J. B., *Behaviourism* (London: W. Norton & Co., 1970).

Watt, Montgomery, *The Influence of Islam on Medieval Europe* (Edinburgh: Edinburgh University Press, 1987).

Wolf, S., 'Effects of Suggestion and Conditioning on the Action of Chemical Agents on Human Subjects: the Pharmacology of Placebos', *Journal of Clinical Investigation* 29 (1950).

al-Zamakhsharī, *Tafsīr al-Kashshāf* (Cairo: Al-Maktabah al-Tijāriyyah, 1354AH).

al-Zubaydī, Imām Zayn al-Dīn Aḥmad ibn ʿAbd al-Laṭīf, *Mukhtaṣṣ Ṣaḥīḥ al-Bukhārī*, vol. 1 (Beirut: Dār al-Kutub al-ʿIlmiyyah, 1993)

INDEX OF QUR'ANIC CITATIONS

2:20 52
2:25 71
2:32 vii
2:164 65
2:219–220 64
2:255 65, 118
3:190–191 57
3:191 45
6:95–96 100
6:101–103 54
6:103 68
7:201 28
7:31 37
10:101 55
12:105 55, 92
13:12–13 87
15:9 15
16:5 54
16:5–6 57
16:10–11 55
16:12–18 55
17:44 51
17:66 65
17:85 12
20:105 75
21:80 65
23:12–14 59
27:62 117
28:76–82 35
29:20 64
30:7 92
30:9 64
32:7 57
34:46 xi
34:9 56
35:27–28 57, 107
35:28 101
36:36 98
36:38–40 100
36:77 60
37:96 66
42:11 67
45:13 59, 111
51:21 62
51:23 61
51:47 84
55:24 65
55:37 73
56:5 76
56:7 77
59:22–24 54
64:3 60
67:23 59
71:13–16 56
75:1–4 60
77:20–24 60
78:20 76
81:1–14 74
82:3 76
88:17–20 56
91:7–10 61
95:4 60
99:1–2 76
103:1–3 61
112:1–5 53

GENERAL INDEX

Adam, 73, 109
Aḥmad ibn Ḥanbal, 71
ᶜAlī ibn Abī Ṭālib, 96
ᶜalim, 107
Allah, 44, 75, 96, 97, 102; see also God and Creator
alcohol (alcoholism), 19, 35, 36, 37, 46, 107
America, 36, 44; American(s), 37, 41, 109, 115; Americanization, 114, 115
American University of Beirut, 117
angel(s), 33, 59, 67, 72–73, 87
anger, 26, 42, 104; aggression, 104
animals, 2–3, 57, 67, 73, 76, 84, 87, 107, 112
ant, 93, 95–98
anxiety, 25, 37, 39, 41, 42, 47, 81, 82, 104, 105
al-ᶜAqqād, ᶜAbbās Maḥmūd, 15, 16
Archimedes, 18
Aristotle, 12
Armstrong, Karen, 49
ascetics, 43, 58
astronomy, 84, 88, 103
automatic thoughts, 18, 22

babies, 99, 107
Bacon, Francis, 102
al-Balkhī, Abū Zayd, 21, 104–106, 107
Barnard, Christian, 13
barrier (*barzakh*), 69, 70, 72
Bedouin, 30, 87, 105
behaviorism, 2, 3, 4, 5, 7, 8; behaviorists, xii, 2, 3, 4, 6, 10, 17, 19
belief(s), ix, x, 4, 10, 11, 13, 17, 20, 21, 23, 39, 40, 41, 43, 45, 49, 69, 93, 102, 107, 108, 109, 110, 116
believer(s), 26–29, 31, 32, 34, 37, 45, 46, 51, 54, 64, 65, 66, 69, 71, 77, 78, 79, 80, 81, 82, 83, 84, 85, 89, 91, 93, 101
Bengelsdorf, I. S., 37
Benson, Herbert, 38, 40, 41, 44–45, 47, 49, 62, 109, 111
Bilāl, 45
biology, 6, 12, 92, 94; biological sciences, 2, 88; biological determinism, 4–5; biological studies, 88
bird(s), 46, 67, 83, 87, 94, 95
body, 10–13, 21, 25, 26, 28, 38, 39, 40, 50, 56, 62, 68, 70, 72, 77, 85, 94, 95, 104, 105
brain, xii, 4, 10–14, 35, 47, 62, 67, 79, 80, 110, 117
breathing, 23, 40, 46, 84, 105
Briffault, Robert, ix
Buddhism/Buddhists, 40, 45
Burt, Cyril, xi, 7

Capra, Fritjof, 84, 110–111
Carson, R. C., 37
Cartesian, 111

cat, 112
cerebral cortex, 11
chemistry, xii, 2, 5, 39, 88, 103
child, 11, 61, 99–100; children, 3, 46, 75, 83; child-rearing, 82
cholesterol, 38, 41
cleanliness, 37, 46; see also *wuḍūʿ* and *ghusl*
cognition, xi, 25, 29, 31, 32, 34, 78; spiritual (*shuhūd*), xi, 30, 32, 113; insightful (*shuhūd*), 31, 113
cognitive, 1, 4, 5, 7, 8, 9, 11, 14, 15, 17, 18, 20, 22, 23, 29, 36, 38, 40, 50, 64, 71, 85, 114, 116; actions, 26, 27; activity(ies), xiv, 2, 5, 7, 8, 14, 16, 17, 18, 20–23, 27, 28, 38, 39, 40, 43, 80, 104; habits, 23; psychology/psychologists, xii, 2, 9, 15, 16, 17, 18, 20, 22, 23, 104, 116; stage(s), 24, 78; therapy/therapist(s), 18, 20, 22, 24, 26, 104, 116
Companion(s), 33, 45, 89, 90, 112
companionship, 71, 85
computer(s), xv, 4, 7, 8, 42, 62; scientist, 15, 16
concentration, 41, 44, 45, 79, 80, 81, 84
conditioned reflex, 6
conditioning, 3, 6
consciousness, xii, xiv, 2, 4, 7, 8, 14, 36, 41, 110, 116; altered state(s) of, xiv, 1, 50, 118
contentment, 20
creation, xi, xii, xiv, 14, 14, 17, 26, 27, 28, 31, 32, 44, 45, 49, 53, 55, 57, 58, 59, 60, 61, 62, 64, 66, 68, 69, 74, 75, 77, 78, 80, 84, 86, 87, 89, 90, 92, 93, 94, 95, 96, 98, 100, 102, 106, 107, 111–113
Creator, 2, 21, 28, 30, 31, 32, 33, 36, 49, 53, 54, 58, 59, 61, 64, 67, 77, 78, 86, 87, 88, 92, 100, 102, 107, 111; see also Allah and God

Darwin (theory of evolution), 6, 109
Dāūd al-Ṭāʿī, 79
David, 65, 122n
Day of Judgment (Resurrection), 60, 64, 72–73, 74, 75, 77
death, 3, 11–12, 29, 31, 32, 35, 37, 69, 70, 72, 74, 105, 110
depression, 17, 39, 81, 82, 104, 105, 106
dhikr, 27, 113; see also remembrance
divorce, 106
dog(s), 6, 33, 112
dream(s), 62, 69, 117, 118
drug(s), 21, 35, 36, 37, 39, 41, 46, 107, 121n; addict, 19, 81, 120n
Durant, Will, ix

East(ern), ix, xiv, 1, 37, 40, 48, 50, 66, 103
Eccles, John, 4, 10–12
Eckartsberg, Rolf von, 110
ego, 5
Einstein (theory of relativity), 6, 9, 43, 84
Elkadi, Ahmed, 47, 48
emotion(s), xiii, xiv, 17, 18, 19, 20, 21, 23, 25, 26, 27, 28, 29, 38, 40, 43, 47, 57, 61, 80
Epictetus, 40
Euclid, 102
Euphrates, 71
Europe(an), 36, 44, 102, 103, 106, 114

experimental science/scientists, xi, xii, 2, 6, 7, 92–112
extrovert(s), 79–81

faith, xii, xiii, 9, 17, 18, 20, 21, 24, 37, 40, 42, 44–45, 46, 47, 49, 53, 54, 61, 62, 66, 78–79, 80, 82, 84, 89, 90, 102, 108, 109, 110, 112
fasting, 37, 102
fear(s), xiii, 17, 19, 28, 34, 38, 56, 57, 73, 86, 87, 88, 101, 104, 105, 122n
feeling(s), xii, xiii, 2, 4, 5, 7, 8, 17, 18, 19, 20, 22, 24, 25, 29, 30, 31, 32, 35, 40, 42, 43, 47, 50, 51, 54, 57, 59, 66, 74, 78, 80, 84, 86, 87, 112
fleeting thoughts, 22–23
fornication, 36, 46
Fried, Paul, 38
Freud, 4, 115, 120n; Freudian psychoanalysis, 4, 5, 115
fiṭrah, 109

Galileo, 102, 108
Gestalt psychology, 6, 93, 117; see also psychology
al-Ghazālī, Abū Ḥāmid, xiv, 6, 14, 21, 25–27, 29–30, 68, 70, 79, 94, 99
al-Ghazālī, Muḥammad, 33
ghusl, 37, 46; see also cleanliness and *wuḍūʾ*
God, x, xi, xii, xiii, xiv, 2, 3, 12, 15, 20, 22, 23, 24, 26, 27, 28, 30, 31, 32, 34, 35, 44, 45, 46, 47, 48, 49, 50, 51, 53–63, 64, 65–69, 72–74, 77, 78, 79, 81, 82, 84–94, 98, 100, 101, 102, 106–114, 117, 118; Divine Being, xi, 30, 67, 68, 69, 77; see also Allah and Creator
grasshopper, 96, 98
grave, 69, 72

habit(s), 16, 18, 19, 20, 21–24, 26, 31, 53, 90, 105, 114
hadith(s), 107, 113; *ḥadīth qudsī,* 70
Hamann, Cecil, 94
happiness, 20, 27, 50, 106, 111
Harre, R., 115
ḥasad, xiii
al-Ḥasan al-Baṣrī, 27, 31, 50, 58, 108
health, 21, 26, 37, 38, 39, 40, 46, 47, 62, 81, 104, 105; psychological, 37, 43, 81, 104
heart(s), 13, 14, 38, 39; (as *qalb*), xiv, 14, 21, 25, 26, 27, 28, 29, 31, 32, 50, 51, 53, 54, 55, 56–57, 59, 62, 72, 73, 74, 84, 87, 88, 94, 113
hereafter, 3, 24, 28, 29, 33, 34, 35, 36, 45–46, 57, 64, 69–72, 74, 77, 92, 101, 107
Hijrah, 112
Hinduism, 45; Hindu(s), 40, 41
Hippocrates, 38
homosexuality, 5
hope, 86, 87, 110
human sciences, x, xii, 88
Hunke, Sigrid, 102
hypochondria, 81

Ibn al-Haytham, 102, 107, 112
Ibn al-Jawzī, 87
Ibn Masʿūd, 68, 71
Ibn al-Qayyim, 21–24, 31, 51, 85–86, 97–98
Ibn Sīnā, 6, 103, 107

Ibn Taymiyyah, 32, 51
Ibn ʿAbbās, xi, 68, 69, 72
imagination, 21, 25, 29, 30, 49, 72, 75, 96
insects, 95, 98
insomnia, 37
interaction (*ishtibāk*), 104
introvert(s), 79–81
invocation (*duʿā*), 117
al-Irgisoosi, Muhammad Khair, 48
Islam, ix, xii, 1, 12, 15, 16, 18, 21, 36, 49, 53, 58, 59, 65, 66, 92, 94, 103, 107, 109, 116; Islamic, vii, viii, ix, x, xi, xiv, 1, 2, 5, 7, 8, 10, 13, 20, 28, 29, 30, 31, 33, 36, 37, 45, 46, 48, 49, 50, 53, 54, 58, 66, 67, 81, 82, 85, 104, 106, 108, 109, 116
Islamization, vii, 108;
of knowledge, x
iḥsān, xi

Jābir ibn Ḥayyān, 112
al-Jundī, Anwar, 16

Kaʿba, 33
Khartoum, xv, 83
khawāṭir, 22–24
Khaybar, 87
khushūʿ, xiii
Kraepelin, Emil, 106
Kuhn, Thomas, 8
al-Khwarazmī, 112

language, xiii, 3, 6, 15–16, 29, 36, 46, 93, 94, 95, 97, 98
le Bon, Gustave, ix
Le Shan, L., 42–43, 49
lesbianism, 5
loneliness, 39, 80
love, xiii, 3, 6, 20, 29, 34, 54, 55, 78, 82, 86, 87, 88, 89, 100, 110, 111, 112, 113
lust (*shahwah*), 23

Madinah, 33, 66, 112
Maḥmūd, Muṣṭafā, 95
Makkah, 66, 87
Malpass, L., 93
mantra, 41
materialists, xii, 10, 11
Mawdūdī, Abūl Aʿlā, 45
medicine, 21, 36, 38, 40, 103
meditation, xi, xiv, 1, 14, 21, 25, 30, 31, 35–52, 59, 64, 77, 78, 79, 81, 82, 84, 86, 91, 95, 101, 102, 107
memory, 8, 18, 23, 47, 61, 62, 71
mind(s), xii, xiv, 2, 4, 7–8, 10–15, 18, 21, 22, 24, 27, 28, 38, 40, 44, 49, 50, 53, 61, 64, 66, 67, 68, 69, 70, 72, 74, 77, 78, 81, 86, 87, 90, 92, 99, 100, 109, 110, 111, 112, 113, 116, 119n
Miskawayh, 21
Moghaddam, F., 115
moon, 55, 56, 58, 60, 69, 73, 79, 96, 97, 100, 112
Moses, 33, 34
mosque(s), 33, 34, 35, 107, 117
mosquito, 99
Mount Uhud, 112
al-Muḥāsibī, al-Ḥārith, 72, 74
murīd, 85
Muslim(s), x, xi, xiii, 1, 12, 17, 20, 21, 23, 25, 26, 32, 33, 36, 37, 44, 45, 46, 47, 50, 51, 66, 69, 71, 82, 89, 90, 92, 93, 101, 102, 104, 108, 111, 112, 113, 114, 116, 118; scholar(s), ix, x, 6, 21–35, 24, 74, 94, 95, 96, 98, 103, 108, 113, 116, 117;

societies, 82, 106, 107; world, ix, 66, 101, 102, 106
mystic(s), 43, 49, 50, 110

nafs, x, xiv, 85
Najati, Muhammad Othman, x
neo-Muᶜtazilites, 89
neuropsychiatry, 4, 5
neurosis, 4, 104–106; neurotic(s), 17, 18, 81, 105, 107, 116
Newton, 43; Newtonian physics, 9, 101, 110
Noah, 56

obsessions, 81, 104
Omdurman, 83
Omdurman Radio, 11

pagan religions, 32–33
pain, 19, 50, 72
Pantheon, 33
paradigm(s), vii, 6, 8–9, 110; behavioristic, 116, 118; paradigm shift, 8, 9
Pavlov, Ivan, 3, 6
Pearce, Joseph, 13–14
philosophy, ix, 12
photosynthesis, 9, 29
physics xii, 2, 5, 6, 9, 12, 30, 43, 84, 85, 102, 103, 110; quantum physics, 43, 101; Newtonian physics, see Newton
pleasures, 17, 71, 106
poetry, xiii, 16, 27, 82
Popper Karl, 11
pregnancy, 38, 39, 76
Prophet Muhammad, x, xi, xiii, 12, 32, 33, 37, 44, 45, 46, 48, 68, 70, 71, 81–82, 85, 89, 90, 101, 102, 107, 108, 112, 113, 119n
pseudocyesis, 38
psyche(s), x, 20, 26, 28, 56, 67, 104
psychoanalysis, 4, 6–7, 116; see also Freud: Freudian psychoanalysis
psychology, vii, x, xi, xii, 1–9, 17, 20, 21, 22, 24, 39, 61, 85, 88, 104, 114–116, 118; psychologists, x, 3, 5, 7, 10, 16, 17, 18, 22, 23, 93, 99, 114, 115, 117, 118; of religion, 1; social, 6, 85; see also Gestalt psychology
psychophysiological, 36, 40, 42, 43, 46, 104
psychosis, 81, 104, 106
psychosomatic, 38, 104
psychotherapy, 104–105, 114–116; psychotherapists, 17, 116
Ptolemy, 102

qalb, see heart
Qārūn, 34–35
Qur'an, vii, x, xi, xii, xii, xiii, 11, 15, 16, 21, 23, 24, 28, 33, 34, 45, 46, 47, 48, 51, 52, 53, 54, 55, 57–61, 64, 66, 67, 70, 76, 77, 83, 84, 86, 92, 98, 100–101, 111, 113, 117, 118, 122n; Qur'anic, 37, 47, 53, 56, 59, 61, 82, 107
Quṭb, Sayyid, 58, 62, 74, 111

al-Rabīᶜ ibn Khaytham, 71
reciprocal inhibition, 19, 24
relaxation, 40, 42, 44, 46, 48
religion, ix, xiv, 1, 3, 4, 5, 17, 33, 45, 47, 66, 85, 92, 102, 106, 107, 108, 109, 110, 116
remembrance, 26, 27, 28, 30, 31, 44, 48, 50, 51, 58, 81, 88, 91, 107, 108, 113, 114; see also dhikr

repetition, 41, 44, 45, 87
revelation, xii, 12, 15, 27; see also Qur'an

sadness, 82, 104, 105, 106
salah, 44, 102, 113, 117
Sarton, George, ix
Satan, 23, 28, 50
scientific method, 92, 101, 102, 110
scientists, 10, 15, 16, 37, 39, 84, 92, 93, 94, 100, 102, 107, 108, 109, 111, 112, 116, 117, 118
Scott Peck, M., 108, 111
secularization, 3, 4, 108; secular, 1, 8, 10, 24, 28, 45, 106, 109, 110, 111, 115, 116, 117, 118
sensory perception, xi, 15, 30, 34, 44, 93
shaykh, 26, 85; see also spiritual master
shirk, 53
shuhūd, vii, x, 30, 113; see also cognition: spiritual
sign(s) of God, xii, 32, 53, 55–56, 57, 59, 60, 62, 64, 65, 66, 87, 92, 97, 102, 111, 121n
social sciences, ix, 8, 9, 39, 88
sodomy, 36, 46
sorrow/distress (*ghummah*), 73, 106, 117, 122n
soul(s), x, xii, xiv, 4, 7, 10, 11, 12, 14, 20, 21, 25, 28, 29, 32, 33, 34, 60, 61, 62, 63, 67, 68, 70, 72, 74, 77, 86, 87, 88, 104, 105, 106, 107, 108, 109, 111, 117; tranquil soul, 85
spirit (*rūḥ*), xiv, 12, 28, 61, 109
spiritual, viii, ix, xii, xiv, 2, 4, 5, 7, 8, 9, 20, 22, 24, 27, 31, 36, 40, 41, 45–48, 51, 54, 62, 66, 85, 86, 88, 89, 90, 95, 98, 106, 107, 108, 113, 114, 116, 117, 122n; state, 50, 53, 78, 81; cognition, xi, 30, 31, 32, 113; contemplation, 14, 24; knowledge, x; practice, 50; spirituality, 12, 29
spiritual master, 85; see also shaykh
stimuli, xi, 2, 4, 5, 6, 8, 10, 17, 40, 79, 80, 93, 116
stress, 19, 37–39, 41, 42, 47, 48
Sufyan al-Thawrī, 27
suicide, 106, 107
sujūd, 117
Sunnah, x, xii, 21, 24, 37, 46

tafakkur, vii, x, xiv, 1, 113
tawḥīd, 53
technology, 8, 14, 66, 89
Temple of Amon, 33
Temple of Jupiter, 33
Third World, 114, 115
thoughts, xiv, 2, 4, 18, 19, 21, 22–24, 26, 27, 29, 29, 31, 41, 62, 86, 104, 116; see also automatic thoughts and fleeting thoughts
al-Tijānī, Yūsuf Bashīr, 14
tranquillity, 20, 24, 42, 47, 81, 82, 100, 113
transcendental meditation, xi, 36, 40, 41, 42, 48

ʿUmar ibn ʿAbd al-ʿAzīz, 58, 108
Ummah, x
unbelievers, 31, 56, 66, 113
unhappiness, 106
University of Khartoum, 48
unseen, xi, 66, 70, 74
Uttal, W., 12, 14

Valle, Ronald, 110

waswasah, 23, 104; see also obsessions
Watson, J. B., xi, 2–3
Watt, W. Montgomery, 103
West, ix–x, xi, xii, 1, 37, 44, 102–103; Western(ers), ix–x, 1, 3, 5, 7, 8, 9, 21, 40, 45, 48, 49, 50, 66, 83, 102, 106, 107, 108, 109, 110, 111, 114, 115, 116, 117, 118
Whitehead, Alfred North, 93
wisdom, 26, 27, 31, 36, 62, 85, 99, 100, 102, 118
Wolf, S., 39
worship, vii, xi, xiv, 1, 17, 21, 27, 32, 34, 36, 37, 45, 46, 48–51, 53, 54, 58, 64–66, 67, 90, 101, 108, 113; worshipper(s), 12, 20, 27, 30, 31, 34, 43, 44, 50, 51, 58, 71, 72, 79, 81, 85, 86, 94, 97, 98, 99, 100, 107, 113, 116, 117
wuḍū', 37, 46; see also cleanliness
yaghbiṭ, xiii
yoga, 40
Yūsuf ʿAlī, 55

al-Zamakhsharī, 98
Zaqqūm, 72